Library of
Davidson College

SOCIAL SCIENCE AND REVOLUTIONS

Revolutions have been a major force in shaping the modern world; an understanding of their causes and nature is vital in order to comprehend historical and contemporary patterns of domestic and international politics. Traditionally, the study of revolutions was viewed mainly, if not exclusively, as the province of normative political theorists or of historians but, following the Cuban revolution, political violence in the West in the 1960s and the 1970s, and American involvement in Vietnam, social scientists became interested in the explanation of revolutions and produced new theoretical and empirical accounts.

In this book Stan Taylor surveys the most important of these contributions deriving from sociological, socio-psychological, economic and political approaches to revolutions. He concludes by rejecting the arguments that social scientific studies of revolutions cannot be differentiated from normative or historical studies, although he suggests that their distinctiveness is a matter of degree rather than of kind. In this sense he argues that the social scientific enterprise, however flawed, has added to the sum of knowledge about revolutions.

Stan Taylor is Lecturer in Politics at the University of Warwick. He is the author of *The National Front in English Politics* and has published a number of articles in academic journals including the *British Journal of Political Science*, *New Community* and the *Sociological Review*.

By the same author

THE NATIONAL FRONT IN ENGLISH POLITICS

SOCIAL SCIENCE AND REVOLUTIONS

Stan Taylor

St. Martin's Press   New York

© Stan Taylor 1984

All rights reserved. For information, write:
St. Martin's Press, Inc., 175 Fifth Avenue, New York, NY 10010
Printed in Hong Kong
First published in the United States of America in 1984

ISBN 0-312-73495-6

Library of Congress Cataloging in Publication Data

Taylor, Stan, 1948–
  Social science and revolutions.

  Bibliography: p.
  Includes index
  1. Revolutions. 2. Social sciences—Research.
I. Title.
HM281.T35   1983   303.6'4   82-19431
ISBN 0-312-73495-6

To my wife

Contents

Acknowledgements		ix
Introduction		1
1	Sociological Theories of Revolutions	10
2	Socio-psychological Theories of Revolutions	52
3	Economic Theories of Revolutions	93
4	Political Theories of Revolutions	114
5	Social Science and Revolutions	151
Notes and References		159
Bibliography		168
Index		174

Acknowledgements

This book is based upon a course in Social Science and Revolutions which I have taught at the University of Warwick since 1974, and I am grateful to successive generations of students who have stimulated discussion on the causes and nature of revolutions. In particular, thanks are due to John Street and Stephen Thomas, both of whom contributed suggestions as to how theories of revolutions should be evaluated. The third chapter is based upon papers given at the University of East Anglia in December 1980 and at the University of Warwick in January 1980. The constructive criticisms of those who discussed the drafts of the chapter caused me to substantially revise my evaluation of the economic theories of revolutions. The final draft was typed by Mrs Gillian Chiles, who succeeded, under considerable pressure, in producing an ordered manuscript from the much-altered chapters given to her. I alone am responsible for the content of the finished product and any errors it may contain.

I would like to acknowledge the permission of the following to quote from copyright material: Professor H. Eckstein and the Free Press *(Internal Wars)*; David Bell and Houghton Mifflin *(Resistance and Revolution)*; James Davies and Signet Books *(Violence in America)*; David McLellan and Macmillan *(Marxism after Marx)*; Barrington Moore Jnr and Allen Lane *(The Social Origins of Dictatorship and Democracy)*; and Professor Charles Tilly and Addison-Wesley *(From Mobilization to Revolution)*.

The purpose of this book is to outline and evaluate the major theories of revolutions produced by social scientists in the 1960s and the 1970s: as such it is a book about other books. It is appropriate to acknowledge the original contributions made by those whose work is discussed, and to express the hope that the necessary condensation of theories and selection of the more important among the strands of arguments has been accomplished without undue simplification of the richness and variety of their work.

My wife has provided advice and encouragement; my two sons have shown forbearance and patience. Without them, this book could not have been written.

S. T.

Introduction

The word 'revolution' derives from the late Latin coinage 'revolutio'. It was originally used by astronomers to describe the lawful, inevitable rotation of the planets: a revolution was a progression from a starting point through an orbit which returned to the point of origin.[1] The word appears to have been first employed as a description of socio-political phenomena during the fourteenth century when 'revoluzione' was used to designate the unexpected, violent and rapid replacement of elites in some of the Italian city states. Hatto[2] has suggested that this usage was related to the revival of astrology in medieval Italy, in that the demise of established elites was held to be associated with sudden and violent changes in the heavens which occurred at certain conjunctions of the revolutions of the planets. Such revolutions were held to be inevitable, beyond the power of man to influence. In the seventeenth century, revolution was applied to socio-political phenomena in a sense more closely allied to its original scientific meaning; it was used to refer to the completion of an historical cycle by which a society had changed from one regime to another – the transition involving violence – and then returned to its original state. Thus the rising of the Portuguese against Spanish domination in 1547 was described by contemporaries as a revolution in that it aimed to restore Portugal's independence;[3] the English Civil War was a revolution in so far as the cycle had begun with monarchy, proceeded to the violent establishment of a republic, and ended with the restoration of the monarchy;[4] the 'Glorious Revolution' in England in 1688–9 was the culmination of a process by which a nominally-Protestant monarch, Charles II, was succeeded by a pro-Catholic king, James II, who was then overthrown and the Protestant ascendancy re-established in the persons of William and Mary.[5] Thus by the mid-eighteenth century, revolution had become part of the political vocabulary used to describe elite replacement, and had variously acquired the connotations of suddenness, violence, inevitability and change ultimately reversed by return to the status quo ante.

The word acquired new meanings during and following the French Revolution which began in 1789. This involved not just the replacement of an elite, but an attempt to implement wholesale changes in the values, norms, structures, roles and environment of society. Further, these changes were perceived not just in the context of contemporary France, but as providing a model for other countries to follow. The implications of this for the concept of revolution may be seen in a comment by the English revolutionary, Tom Paine, who wrote in 1791:

> What we formerly call revolutions were little more than a change of persons, or an alteration of local circumstances. They rose and fell like things of course, and had nothing in their existence or fate that could influence them beyond the spor that produced them. But what we now see in the world . . . are a renovation of the natural order of things, a system of principles as universal as truth and the existence of man, and combining moral with political happiness and natural prosperity.[6]

The quote illustrates the extent to which revolution became associated with social restructuring of a universally-applicable kind, but Paine still retained some of the older meaning of the word by specifying that revolutions involved renovation, a return to an actual or a mythical past. The abandonment of this and the development of the notion that revolutions embodied progress in sense is most strongly associated with Hegel.[7] Revolution to Hegel was the revelation of the dialectic of history, of the process by which an existing society and its negation were synthesised into an order which embodied both and yet transcended them to create a new form of society which was held to mark a qualitative progression in the development of the world. It was in this sense that revolution was used by Marx,[8] although in his formulation the dialectical process was not a metaphysical one, but one anchored in concrete economic, social and political relations between men. Marx postulated a model of societal development which depended upon a series of dynamic relationships between the technological state of a society, its economic organization, and the social and political structures to which the latter gave rise.

Revolution was the process by which the tensions arising from the existence of discrete technologies, forms of economic ownership and appropriate social and political arrangements were finally resolved through class conflict; it occurred when one class displaced another to establish a society in which socio-political relations were conducive to the development of a particular technology associated with a given form of resource ownership. By the late nineteenth century, then, the older meaning of revolution had been complemented by new notions of the scope, universality, direction and nature of the kinds of changes involved.

The particular meaning of the word employed has implications in tracing the history of revolutions which have taken place and in outlining the development of the concept of revolution in social and political thought. If the older connotations of the word, or derivatives of them, are used, then revolutions may be variously found in Ancient Egypt,[9] classical Greece and Rome,[10] medieval[11] and early modern[12] Europe, as well as in the First, Second and Third Worlds from the eighteenth century onwards. On this basis discussions of revolutions have been held to be present in the works of, for example, Plato,[13] Aristotle,[14] Thucydides[15] and Machiavelli,[16] as well as more recent social and political theorists. If the later definition is used, revolutions are a more modern phenomena, beginning variously with the English Civil War[17] or the American War of Independence[18] or the French Revolution.[19] The theorists writing prior to the seventeenth century were analysing sub-revolutionary phenomena such as resistance, rebellion and revolt, and consideration of revolution can be said to have started with Locke[20] or Burke[21] and continued through De Tocqueville,[22] Hegel, Marx and the last's followers.[23]

Whatever the merits of one definition compared to another, there can be little doubt that there have been more revolutions of any kind during the twentieth century than in any other period in recorded history, and that these have had greater impact upon a larger number of states and societies than in earlier centuries. The history of the century could be written around the revolutions which occurred in Russia, Italy, China, Cuba, Algeria and Vietnam which directly or indirectly stimulated communist, socialist, fascist, nationalist and anti-colonial revolutions or counter-revolutions throughout the world and in the process changed the patterns of domestic and international politics in every country of the world. There is a considerable consensus[24] that, if any century deserves the title of the 'century of revolution', it is the present one.

It would be expected that the study of revolutions would have been a central focus of the social sciences as they developed in the twentieth century, given the number and importance of revolutions as well as the existence of a tradition of analysis of the subject stretching back at least to the seventeenth century and possibly to antiquity. Surprisingly, social scientists accorded relatively little attention to revolutions prior to 1960. This was despite the lead given to the development of the topic by Pitrim Sorokin, an exile from Russia, who held a Chair at Harvard and who published *The Sociology of Revolution* in 1925 and followed this up with a second study[25] which appeared in 1938. The only other serious books which were wholly or largely devoted to the general analysis of revolutions were those of Le Bon (1913),[26] Edwards (1927),[27] Pettee[28] and Brinton[29] (both published in 1938), Chorley (1943),[30] Brogan (1951),[31] Lasswell and Kaplan (1955)[32] and Gross (1958);[33] in addition to this there were a few articles in journals, notably by Ellwood (1905),[34] Yoder (1926),[35] Riezler (1943),[36] Gottshalk (1944),[37] Hatto[38] and Neumann[39] (both 1949), Hopper (1950),[40] Deutscher (1952),[41] Palmer (1954)[42] and Wallace (1956)[43]. This literature was minimal compared to that produced in almost any other area of social scientific enquiry over the same period. It may be noted that Freeman[44] has termed these studies collectively the 'second wave' of studies of revolutions, the first wave comprising the contributions of the various social and political theorists mentioned earlier.

This neglect of the study of revolutions would be comprehensible if social scientists had been interested in problems which had little or no relevance to the subject. However, as Eckstein[45] has suggested, the reverse was the case: the 'grand' problems of social science centred around the determinants of social stability and instability, of social conflict and its resolution, and there was a wealth of theories purporting to explain and analyse the nature and causes of differential patterns of societal change. He expressed the apparent paradox between the concerns of social science and the lack of attention to revolutions in that:

> Rarely, it seems, have social thinkers been so well equipped with basic concepts, perspectives, and analytical approaches

designed to make sense of the phenomena of internal war. Their literature teems with the requisites for social order, functional imperatives for solidary social life, and theories of social interaction and communication, effective and ineffective socialization, alienation and aggression. One would think that anyone interested in social solidarity, integration, equilibrium and conformity – the grand theoretical problems of contemporary social science – would be consumingly interested in their ultimate negation in revolutionary conflict. And one would have thought that any theory meant to illuminate the one set of conditions could be applied, without much change and difficulty, to its opposite.[46]

Eckstein tried to explain this paradox by reference to the theoretical and methodological orientations of the social sciences. Firstly, he suggested that the penchant for 'over-arching theory'[47] – for producing all-inclusive macro-level frameworks for analysis of societies of the kind associated with the name of Parsons[48] in sociology – had resulted in the creation of a body of theory which was difficult to apply to concrete cases of social change such as revolutions. His second point was that the nature of revolutions was such as to inhibit the deployment of empirical methodologies then in vogue in the social sciences. While it was possible to produce quantitative data on (say) electoral behaviour without too much difficulty, revolutionary behaviour was not amenable to the same kind of treatment, and had been neglected because the available data was of a lower order than social scientists regarded as acceptable. With the benefit of hindsight, neither of these arguments are particularly convincing; social scientists have adapted 'grand' theory to the explanation of revolutions and produced analyses using quantitative data to illuminate the causes and nature of revolutions, as will be seen.

A rather different explanation has been presented by Pye.[49] Violence and insurgency had a 'fundamentally shocking and disturbing character'. The study of revolutionary phenomena recalled past hurtful traumas which had been repressed into the subconscious minds of members of societies. Researching revolutions was then a psychologically-painful process compared to researching other social and political phenomena, and the costs thus imposed inhibited the development of the subject.

This argument is difficult to accept in view of one point: the most traumatic experience of any group during the present century was that of the extermination of the Jews during the Second World War, but this appeared if anything to stimulate Jewish academics to undertake research on the social, economic and political conditions which had made the Holocaust possible.[50] Indeed, it can be argued that Pye's argument should be reversed: the lack of studies of revolutions may have stemmed from the fact that most social scientists lived in the Anglo-American democracies – with the highest concentration in the United States – where there were no traumas of political violence in recent memory to promote the study of the subject.

The last interpretation appears to be consistent with the circumstances surrounding the burgeoning of interest in political violence and revolutions which took place in the United States during the 1960s and early 1970s. During the 1950s most Americans had perceived that (1) the United States was a society in which great conflicts over class, status and power had been resolved by a judicious combination of a welfare state, decentralized decision-making, a mixed economy and political pluralism[51] and (2) its international role towards the developing world was one of paternal assistance in promoting the conditions under which poor countries could seek to emulate the American example.[52] Violence and revolution were a matter of domestic history or internationally the consequences of the inability of the decaying European powers to accept the loss of their empires or Soviet subversion. The study of such phenomena could be safely left to historians or military specialists. These images were rudely shattered at the very end of the 1950s and during the 1960s and early 1970s by the emergence of domestic violence and conflict – the assassinations of President Kennedy, Senator Kennedy and Martin Luther King, the black riots and the student revolts – and by American involvement in counter-revolution throughout Latin America and in Asia, particularly of course in Vietnam.

These events had an impact upon American social scientists in four ways. Firstly, academic curiosity about the causes and nature of political violence and revolutions was aroused. It is significant that the first major conference[53] on 'internal war' held in the postwar period was promoted by the Centre for International Studies at Princeton in 1960, the year after the successful revolution against the American-backed regime in Cuba, the island lying only ninety miles from the mainland of the United States. Subsequent developments – the attempt to promote counter-revolution in Cuba in 1961, the missile crisis of 1962 and the export of the Cuban revolution to other Latin American countries in the early 1960s – affirmed the importance of revolution as a factor in world politics. This was recognized in 1963 when the American Political Science Association for the first time organized a panel on violence and revolution at its Annual Meeting. The burning of cities during the black riots, and American involvement in South East Asia similarly stimulated an interest in revolutions. The second factor was that government funding became available for research into the subject. In 1963 the Defence Department sponsored a large-scale study of violence and revolution,[54] although this ultimately collapsed because of differing interpretations of the aims of the research by the Department and by the social scientists involved. Research funds also became available to examine domestic political violence, in particular through the National Commission on the Causes and Prevention of Violence.[55] A third influence was academic opposition to the Vietnam war. Military interventions by the United States had traditionally been viewed as the Second World arbitrating the disputes of the First World (Europe) or of the Third World in the interests of liberty and democracy. However, the justice of American involvement in Vietnam was widely questioned in the mid- and late-1960s, not least by a number of academic social scientists, some of whom became active in the anti-war movement. This activism in itself encouraged the exploration of the causes and nature of violence and revolution. The final factor was perhaps the most important stimulus to the study of revolutions, and this was the interest in the topic generated among students. Bell has outlined the influence of domestic violence in the United States upon 1960s students as follows:

> As long as the American political system was (or appeared to be) functioning 'normally' . . . college students in the 1950s ignored it almost completely . . . In the next decade, all this changed dramatically. Students vaulted from apathy to involvement. Politics became the hottest issue on the campus. The image of politics as a well-oiled, smoothly-functioning

machine appeared ludicrous against the backdrop of burning cities.[56]

Student radicalism, and a desire to learn about revolution and violence, was further fuelled by opposition to conscription and to the Vietnam war, as well as by the responses to such opposition by the regime, particularly the violence which attended the Democratic Party convention in 1968 and the shooting of students at Kent State University in 1972. College students demanded that their courses should take account of what they saw as the realities of the world, and that research opportunities should be made available to study revolutions. These demands met with a generally positive response,[57] and helped to encourage research and teaching in the field.

The consequence of these developments was the publication of a number of books and articles in which social scientists of various disciplinary persuasions attempted to use the conceptual and methodological tools of the social sciences to explain the incidence and nature of political violence and revolutions. The central concern of the present book is the exposition and evaluation of the major contributions among these 'third wave' studies of revolutions. The rationale for writing it was twofold. Firstly, two decades had passed since the Princeton conference launched the new study of revolutions, and it seemed appropriate to examine and assess the most important products of this research enterprise. Secondly, it was thought to be a useful exercise to collate a disparate literature within a single book to provide for the needs of undergraduates or postgraduates taking courses wholly or partly concerned with revolutions. Students could be pointed to Cohen's[58] introductory text, or to the review articles of Freeman,[59] Stone[60] or Zagorin,[61] but these were only partial in their coverage and, by the early 1980s, outdated by new accounts.

This book is not intended to be completely comprehensive in its coverage of the post-1960 literature on theories of revolutions: this task would require publication in several volumes. Rather, a number of theories have been selected which are, in the author's opinion, the most important recent contributions to the study of revolutions, and which illustrate the diversity of approaches to the subject among the social science fraternity. In order to reflect the different ways in which social scientists have approached the analysis of revolutions, the various studies have been grouped according to the dominant disciplinary perspective employed, and within this by particular theoretical orientations, where appropriate. Thus in Chapter 1, sociological theories are considered under the sub-headings of 'functionalist' and 'class conflict' approaches; the second chapter is concerned with aggregate-psychological theories, subdivided into those emphasizing 'cognitive dissonance' and those based in the 'frustration–aggression–violence' matrix; in Chapter 3, the work of three theorists employing 'economic' or 'rational choice' approaches to revolutions is discussed; and in the fourth chapter theories deriving from 'political functionalist' and 'political conflict' conceptual frameworks are considered. In the final chapter, an attempt is made to evaluate the contribution of these theories to the understanding of revolutions.

1 Sociological Theories of Revolutions

The central contention of sociological theories was that the causes of revolutions could be located primarily in the dynamics of social relations between members of society.[1] Such theories involved a major stress upon social systems, social institutions and social stratification, although this did not preclude the use of related economic, cultural, political or psychological explanatory variables. Within this overall orientation, the sociological theories diverged in their approach to revolution, reflecting their origins in two different strands of socio-political thought, namely functionalism and conflict-coercion theory.[2] These constituted quite different approaches to a common problem, the description and analysis of societal stability and instability.

The functionalist approach, which was most closely associated with Durkheim,[3] Parsons[4] and Merton,[5] was based in the proposition that the chances of stability in any given society were, in the long run, dependent upon the extent to which there was a consensus among its members as to the goals it should pursue and the means of implementing such goals. This, in turn, was held to be determined by the success or otherwise of the social system of a society in fulfilling a number of functions which promoted support for the status quo. While these functions included the use of coercion to sustain support, this was only held to provide a short-term solution to the emergence of significant discontent which, if unalleviated, ultimately led to social action to reconstitute the social system in a different form. In this context, the study of revolutions involved analysis of the ways in which a social system failed to fulfil its functions to the extent that there was a mass mobilization to create a new system which could adequately maintain stability. The most noted theorist utilizing this approach was Johnson,[6] whose work is considered in the first part of this chapter.

The basic premise of the conflict-coercion approach was that the key to understanding social stability lay in an appreciation of the conflict embodied in societies by virtue of the existence of inequalities between members and groups of members in the actual or potential possession of economic and power resources and hence in the present or future rewards flowing from resource ownership. The presence of such inequalities, and their persistence over time, meant that social conflict was endemic in societies. Dominant groups could try to ensure that this remained latent by deploying various mechanisms of social control, but stability ultimately depended upon the threat or actuality of coercion. This perspective was, of course, apparent in the writings of Marx, and implied that the study of revolutions should be directed towards the analysis of the relations between groups competing for resources in the context of how these influence the ability of dominant groups to contain conflict. The work of two theorists, Barrington Moore[7] and Skocpol,[8] which was grounded in this approach, is considered in the second part of this chapter.

JOHNSON AND THE SOCIOLOGICAL FUNCTIONALIST APPROACH TO REVOLUTIONS

Given both the stability of the Anglo-American democracies up to the 1960s and the concentration of sociologists within those countries, particularly the United States, it is not particularly surprising that the functionalist perspective was so pervasive among sociologists in the early postwar period. The countries in which the vast bulk of sociologists lived, worked and researched were, in general, stable, and turmoil was infrequent, short-lived and small-scale enough to be generally ignored. Thus the sociological enterprise became the derivation and application of functionalist theories to the stable societies. This focus had the additional intellectual advantage of permitting the development of social scientific constructs by reference to stable cases, an exercise which, it could be argued, was a necessary preliminary to the extension of theories for the analysis of more complex unstable ones.

The various disturbances in the United States in the 1960s and 1970s alluded to in the Introduction brought about a reappraisal of the functionalist approach among sociologists. Some rejected it outright:[9] others attempted to show that functionalism was adequate as a conceptual tool in analysing instability as well as stability. Among the latter was Smelser,[10] who utilized a functionalist approach to explain 'collective behaviour', in which was included panics, crazes, hostile outbursts and support for norm-oriented and value-oriented movements. Smelser devoted some attention to revolutions but, as Freeman has shown,[11] this was only a speculative by-product of the general argument and did not constitute a sustained or coherent attempt at explanation of this phenomenon. The major task of adapting functionalism to the case of revolutions was left to Johnson,[12] whose book was published in 1966.

Johnson commenced his analysis with a series of general points concerning the sources and nature of social stability. In all societies there was a division of labour which was associated with hierarchies of economic rewards, power and status. For a society to be stable, its adult members had to accept these inequalities: if they did not, there would be competition, conflict and ultimately instability. In order to promote the acceptance of inequality, there had to be some 'principles that render the division of labour intelligible and tolerable'[13] and which commanded general agreement. Johnson termed these values, and suggested that they had a dual character. On the one hand, they provided explanations for inequalities (for example that Hindu 'untouchables' were such because they had committed crimes in previous incarnations); on the other they were standards of action designed to guide behaviour in such a way as to minimize potential conflict (thus untouchables had to resign themselves to their lowly lot in order to atone for past errors and maximize the chances of later reincarnation in a higher caste). Values of these kinds were incorporated in ideologies, religions, social myths, moral philosophies and metaphysical beliefs and, if these provided adequate reasons for inequalities and appropriate standards of behaviour, social stability would follow. Instability stemmed from values coming to be regarded as illegitimate justifications or mis-specifying the appropriate conduct to keep conflict within manageable bounds.

The task of the social system of a society was to maintain a consensus as to existing values among the population. A social system 'is composed of actions (roles), played from statuses and guided by norms'.[14] Roles were 'obligations and rights which are socially recognised and which, being so recognised, allow (the individual) to determine his own behaviour and to orient himself to the behaviour of others'.[15] Such roles varied according to the individual's social position or status; differential conduct would be expected from (say) a managing director and a production-line worker. Variations in roles not only reflected this, but also norms, 'positive rules of behaviour . . . which are elaborated in accordance with a system's value structure'.[16] Thus, if a society's values included a proscription upon the viewing of women's faces in public, this norm would be applicable to the various social positions filled by women, regardless of whether these were in the boardroom or on the shop floor.

The maintenance of social harmony depended upon the relationship between the values of the society and the components of its social system. Where these were synchronized, to use Johnson's term, stability would result. For example, there would be no threat from Hindu untouchables if they accepted the values governing their situation as legitimate, adhered to prescribed norms of conduct and status expectations and played appropriate roles. If, however, they were induced to reject value explanations of their plight, and acquired exalted status expectations, desynchronization would occur and be associated with instability as untouchables pursued an improvement in their situation. Where synchronization was sustained over time, Johnson described the social system as being in equilibrium; where a system became desynchronized over a period it was designated as being in a state of disequilibrium.

The chances of any social system being in equilibrium or otherwise were determined by the degree to which the system successfully fulfilled a number of functions necessary to its continued survival. Johnson, following Parsons,[17] outlined four such functions. The first was that of socialization, ensuring that the values and norms of the society were effectively transmitted to new members, particularly children and immigrants. The second was adaptation to changes in the environment in which the system operated, particularly changes in the economic system, the importance of which will be seen later. The third function was goal-attainment, the mobilization and allocation of resources to most effectively promote policies, and the production of a consensus that goals would be best achieved by a given distribution of resources. The final function was that of integration and social control, one fulfilled positively by the demonstration of the basic values of the system by dominant groups, individuals and institutions within the society, and negatively by the use of the threat or actuality of force against those who potentially or actually deviated from the existing value-norm-status-role arrangements of the society. The primary agent of this last function was the state which Johnson, following Weber,[18] defined as 'the institutionalised set of roles entrusted with the authoritative exercise of force'.[19]

These various functions had to be performed in the face of four types of change over time. Exogenous value changes were changes induced from outside sources into the value system of a society, for example the 'demonstration effects' of the French, Russian and Cuban Revolutions upon the populations of other countries. Endogenous value changes were internally-induced changes in a society's values, for example attempts to separate church and state during the process of modernization. These sources of change were complemented by changes in the environment of the social system. Exogenous environmental changes occurred in response to external factors, such as the importation of technology which changed the form of agriculture and hence led to wider social and economic change; endogenous environmental changes referred to internal developments such as technical innovations which had an impact upon economic organization and social structure.

Changes of these kinds, Johnson argued, placed considerable strains upon social systems in fulfilling the functions necessary to maintain stability. Some, with long experience, would be able to adapt their performance of existing functions to new circumstances almost automatically, and sustain a homeostatic, or self-regulating, equilibrium. Others would be unable to respond and the resultant dysfunctioning of the social system would lead to desynchronization and, in the longer term, disequilibrium. Such developments were most likely when change was unprecedented, sudden, and very intense. Johnson, at this stage of his analysis, saw two possible outcomes to disequilibrium, namely reform (new policies to resynchronize the social system, correct dysfunction and return to equilibrium) or revolution (whereby these objectives would be achieved by force). He defined the latter formally as 'attempts to realise changes in the constitutions of societies by force',[20] constitutions in this usage referring to social systems and the way in which these were structured to meet functional needs.

The probability of one or other of these outcomes was determined by three factors. The first was the extent to which dysfunction led to a growing reliance by the state upon violence to maintain order, with a consequential loss of legitimacy. Environmental and/or value changes destroyed established relationships between the parts of the social system: this upset the maps of members of society as to how they should behave in social situations. Johnson, utilizing psychological theories of the types discussed in Chapter 3, argued that this led to disorientation and tension among individuals affected by change, which was reflected in rising crime and increased availability for mobilization by extremist movements providing new ideologies which specified alternative means of resynchronizing the social system. Given this, the state was forced to use coercion in order to govern, and increasing resort to violence led to popular questioning of the legitimacy of the state. Johnson described this process as a 'power deflation'.[21] He argued that as long as de-legitimization was limited by the perception that violence was a temporary phase pending the introduction of new policies which would result in a return to equilibrium, the existing society could survive; however, long-term, extensive reliance upon force would eventually lead to a massive power deflation in which popular consent would be withdrawn.

The second factor was that of the effectiveness of elite attempts to realign the social system. Johnson described five kinds of elite responses: intransigence, carrying on as usual, conservative change, the co-option of disaffected groups, and elite abdication. He saw the first and last responses as associated with revolution. Intransigence would fuel power deflation; elite abdication would leave the door open for revolutionary movements to capture the state. These responses would not, however, necessarily lead to revolution. Johnson suggested that systems with intransigent elites suffering from power deflation could survive (by creating a police state as in South Africa[22]) or that elite abdication could be followed by an agreed, orderly and peaceful transfer of power.[23] It may be noted that the admission of the South African case provides a third alternative outcome of disequilibrium, although Johnson himself does not appear to recognize this.

For intransigence or abdication to be followed by revolution, a third condition had to be met, namely the presence of 'some ingredient, usually contributed by fortune, which deprives the elite of its chief weapon for enforcing social behaviour . . . or which leads a group of revolutionaries to believe that they have the means to deprive the elite of its weapons of coercion'.[24] This chance factor opened the door for attempts to overthrow the established elite, i.e. accelerated the mobilization of discontent into revolution. Johnson outlined three types of accelerators. The first referred to factors directly influencing the support of the military for a particular elite, and included the relationship between the military and the wider society (for example, whether or not the officer corps were members of the defending elite), the internal structure of the military (whether or not middle-ranking officers were content with their promotion prospects), and morale (defeat in war destroyed military support for the regime). The second class of accelerators referred to revolutionary elites, which might decide that they had a good chance of defeating the forces defending an elite. Johnson cited as an example the belief of the rebels in the Boxer Rebellion in China that they were immune from bullets, a hypothesis which was quickly falsified when put to the test. The last group of accelerators related to the strategy of revolutionary movements, whether this included the organization of a lightning coup d'état, or a longer guerilla campaign against the military of an established elite. The accelerator itself was the strategic decision that the time was ripe for a coup or a push to military defeat by extending guerilla warfare. Johnson's model of revolution is summarized in Figure 1.1. It can be seen from this that Johnson specified three necessary conditions for revolution to occur – that the social system should be in a state of disequilibrium, that power deflation should be extensive and that elites should respond by intransigence or abdication – and one necessary and sufficient condition, the presence of an accelerator. The absence of the latter meant that, even if the three other conditions were met, non-revolutionary outcomes would result, namely a police state where the elite response was one of intransigence, or a peaceful transfer to a new elite where the regime had abdicated.

This analysis can be subjected to considerable criticism, both within its own terms of reference and in the wider sense of the alleged inapplicability of theories derived from functionalism to the explanation of revolutions. A number of points may be made with reference to Johnson's four conditions for revolution, accepting for the moment the validity of his general approach. Firstly, it is by no means clear that the distinction between social systems in equilibrium or disequilibrium is realistic. Perfectly-functioning synchronized social systems are the stuff of Utopian ideologies; all systems suffer from dysfunctioning and desynchronization to some degree. This implies that the potential for revolution is not dependent upon a distinction of kind between systems in equilibrium or disequilibrium, but a distinction of degree of disequilibrium. In this sense it can be argued that Johnson should have been concerned to specify particular levels of disequilibrium which were critical in determining outcomes rather than dichotomizing the equilibrium variable. There is, in fact, some evidence that Johnson may have appreciated this point at a late stage in his work. The penultimate chapter of his book is concerned with the measurement of degrees of disequilibrium, using suicide rates, crime rates and changes in the strength of the military as statistical indicators. However, as he himself noted,[25] this exercise was unfruitful because there were influences other than the social system upon the variables used to measure

Social system	Power deflation	Elite responses	Accelerator	Outcome
In equilibrium	–	–	–	Homeostatically equilibrating system
In disequilibrium	Limited	Adaptation	–	Resynchronization by existing elite
	Extensive	Intransigence	Yes	Revolution
			No	Police state
		Abdication	Yes	Revolution
			No	Peaceful transfer and resynchronization by new elite

FIGURE 1.1 *Johnson's model of revolution*

disequilibrium. Given this, the operationalization of the system disequilibrium component of his theory is reduced to the status of a 'we know it when we see it' proposition, which is hardly helpful to those seeking to apply his model to particular cases or use it for predictive purposes.

A second criticism of the theory within its own terms concerns the mitigating relationship between disequilibrium and outcomes attributed to varying elite responses. Johnson viewed adaptation or reform as leading to non-revolutionary change in that an existing or a new elite (which had come to power peacefully) introduced new policies which resynchronized the social system. There is, however, a substantial body of research[26] which suggests that, if anything, elite reforms have acted as accelerators of revolution. Reforms variously raised expectations to levels which elites could not attain (thus reducing popular support) or were regarded as demonstrating elite vulnerability (encouraging even more radical demands to be made); a policy of no concessions prevented either of these developments from taking place, and preserved the stability of the system. It is thus possible to suggest that Johnson's specification of the relationship between elite responses and revolution should be reserved.

Johnson could reply to such criticism by claiming that it neglected the impact of elite responses upon power deflation, that the prospect of reform would reduce this while intransigence would result in increased delegitimization of the regime, which would raise the potential for revolution. This riposte, however, is considerably undermined by Johnson's admission that social systems could survive despite massive power deflation, as in South Africa. Clearly if elites were willing and able to create and operate a police state, the extent of power deflation in itself was relatively immaterial to the survival of the system. This point also has implications for the general applicability of functionalist models to revolutions, as will be seen.

These criticisms undermine the status of Johnson's three necessary conditions for revolution, and doubt concerning these is reinforced by the work of Russell.[27] She compared the societies of Cuba and South Africa in the 1950s in terms of relative degrees of disequilibrium of their social systems, the extent of elite intransigence, and levels of power deflation, and concluded that the latter country had a considerably greater potential for revolution than the former. The fact that Cuba had a revolution at the end of this period, and South Africa did not, would seem to suggest that Johnson's model was not universally applicable.

The final component of the model was the specification of the accelerators which were necessary and sufficient conditions of revolution. This, as Freeman has noted,[28] may be challenged on two grounds. Firstly, some of the events defined as accelerators – those classed under the strategy of revolutionary movements – were not accelerators at all, but the consequences of accelerators. Decisions by revolutionary leaders to set a coup in motion or to extend guerilla warfare in a final push for victory were part of the initial phase of revolution: the accelerators were whatever circumstances precipitated such actions. This class of accelerators was not composed of independent variables, but of variables which were part of the dependent variable of revolution which they were supposed to explain. Secondly, there is a difficulty arising from the status of accelerators as 'ingredients, usually contributed by fortune'. This implies that, given a set of societies which fulfilled the necessary conditions for revolution, the chance of the latter occurring in any one case was the same as the chance that the one live round in the spinning chamber of a gun would be opposite the firing pin when the trigger was pressed. Just as the location of the active bullet could only be known by whether or not it was fired, the intervention of fortune could only be adjudged from whether or not a revolution occurred in a particular case. This effectively means that Johnson's proposition concerning the role of accelerators cannot be confirmed or refuted. In order to validate that these were necessary and sufficient conditions for revolutions, it would have to be demonstrated that all accelerator events (or at least those which were not themselves part of revolution) had been followed by revolutions, and that no revolutions had taken place in the absence of an accelerator. In order to do this, a set of accelerator events would have to be defined independently of a set of revolutions, and the degree of matching would have to be established. This task is not possible, given that there is no way of specifying whether events were the product of fortune (and would thus qualify as accelerators) or other factors (in which case they would not) apart from the fact that revolutions had or had not occurred (a revolution revealing the intervention of fortune, non-revolution indicating its absence).

Thus Johnson's necessary and sufficient condition for

revolution would appear in fact to comprise a combination of propositions which came down to a confusion between explanatory and dependent variables and a belief that revolution must reflect the workings of inscrutable providence. Thus if Johnson had tried to rescue part of his theory from Russell's criticisms by arguing that the comparison between Cuba and South Africa illustrated the importance of the vital fourth condition of revolution, which was present in the former and missing in the latter, he would in fact be suggesting that (1) a revolution had happened in Cuba but not in South Africa because a revolution had happened in Cuba but not in South Africa (if he used the 'strategy of revolution' class of accelerators) and/or (2) that fortune had intervened in Cuba, but not South Africa, the evidence for this being that one had had a revolution and the other had not. The first point is tautological, the second theological; neither are acceptable as social scientific theory if this is to have any substantive meaning.

In addition to these problems with Johnson's theory as it stands, a number of other criticisms may be made as to whether the type of approach embodied in the theory is adequate to explain revolutions. Firstly, it has been argued by Eckstein[29] that the systems approach assumes an identity between dysfunction and consequent political behaviour which may not be true. The relationship may be mediated by attitudes, with relatively low degrees of system dysfunction promoting revolution in one society and higher degrees of dysfunction being associated with stability in another, because attitudes towards the permissible extent of dysfunction differ. It is, for example, to be wondered how many other countries would be able to stagger along in apparently perpetual dysfunction, like Italy, without considerably greater political violence than has taken place in that country. The social systems model fails to allow for the influence of 'political culture' in influencing the relationship between dysfunction and violence. Secondly, it is possible to express doubts as to the empirical usefulness of the model in analyzing concrete historical cases of revolutions. It would be, to say the least, a very difficult task for a researcher to describe the set of value-role-norm-statuses in a society, identify varying levels of dysfunction, and operationalize these in relation to other variables in the model. Johnson himself did not attempt this; historians[30] aware of his work have not tried to deploy the full theory, but have only used the distinction made between long-term and proximate causes of revolution as a guideline for their research.

The final criticism is that Johnson's theory characterizes revolutions in a way remote from human experience. Revolutions are described and analyzed using terms and constructs used normally to refer to the behaviour of physical phenomena – systems, structures, dysfunction, desynchronization, acceleration – which renders them apparently abstract, mechanistic events almost autonomous from the real world. There is, as Stone has noted,[31] has noted, little role in the model for the 'operation of the unique and the personal', the personalities and idiosyncrasies of revolutionary actors which may, deliberately or by accident, influence the chances of one outcome or another in a particular case. It can similarly be argued that the clinical, neutral world of system dysfunction serves to obscure the fact that the basis of revolutions is the existence of inequalities in wealth and power between classes in society who struggle for the ownership of the means of production, distribution and exchange. This last perspective is, of course, associated with Marx and those who have attempted to adapt, or amend, his ideas on revolutions.

MARX AND REVOLUTIONS

McLellan has summarized the legacy which Marx considered himself to have bequeathed to posterity in that he had

> shown that the sum total of relations of production – the way men organized their social production as well as the instruments they used – constituted the real basis of society upon which there arose a legal and political superstructure and to which corresponded definite forms of consciousness. Thus, the way men produced their means of subsistence conditioned their whole social, political and intellectual life. But at a certain stage in their evolution the forces of production would develop beyond the relations of production and these would act as a fetter. Such a stage inaugurated a period of social revolution. These productive forces had to develop to the fullest extent possible under the existing relations of production before the old social order would perish. It was possible to pick out the asiatic, ancient, feudal and modern bourgeois modes of

production as progressive epochs in the economic formation of society. These bourgeois relations of production were the last ones to create a divided society and, with their end, the prehistory of human society would be brought to a close. For bourgeois society would end with a period of revolution that would culminate in the proletariat, through the agency of its own political party, gaining power and, after a period of dictatorship, creating a classless, communist society.[32]

This interpretation of Marx as projecting an inexorable progression of societies through successive stages, with the completion of one stage a necessary condition for transformation by social revolution into the next, has been questioned in the light of writings and notes[33] which remained unpublished during his lifetime. However, the various revisions have not significantly altered the perception that Marx expected that the main arena for communist revolutions would be the industrialized nations of the West – particularly Britain, France and Germany[34] – where the dynamic forces promoting capitalist breakdown were most advanced and where the large urban proletariats had already begun to organize for eventual revolution. While Marx did not totally rule out the prospect of socialist revolutions in agrarian societies such as Russia,[35] he was sceptical as to this prospect: the peasantry was at best a reluctant supporter of change, at worst a positive source of conservatism.[36]

Events since Marx's death in 1883 were effectively the reverse of these expectations. The Western capitalist nations remained relatively stable, or were threatened more by fascist than by communist revolution; the latter occurred in backward, predominantly agrarian societies, and received substantive support from the peasantry. This apparent failure of Marx's model to predict patterns of development and revolution in the twentieth century stimulated a debate as to Marx's approach, his conceptualization of variables and his specification of the interrelationships between these. Some theorists[37] rejected Marx's model as a predictive model virtually in its entirety, on the basis that his analysis of capitalism in particular was predicated upon the assumption that trends apparent during his lifetime would be continued and magnified in the process of development; they argued that capitalism had developed into a form unforeseen by Marx, that of industrial society, and this negated his theory.

Other theorists attempted to retain some of Marx's central constructs while allowing for variations in relationships between particular variables or the extension of Marx's theory to cases outside those to which his analysis was originally intended to apply. Academic Marxists or neo-Marxists[38] stressed that the apparent adaptability of capitalism could, in some measure, be explained by allowing for a realm of relative autonomy between the state and the dominant class in capitalist societies. Marx himself said little on this subject: he intended to write a volume on the state, but this project was still outstanding at the time of his death. The perception of Marx's thought which became the orthodoxy was that expressed in the *Communist Manifesto*,[39] that the state was simply an instrument of the dominant class to maintain itself by coercion and social control. However, some Marxists have allowed that this was not entirely the case in contemporary capitalist societies, where the state had played a role in ensuring the survival of capitalism by, in effect, restraining the bourgeoisie from pushing capitalism to its revolutionary grave in the unmitigated pursuit of profit. This was not, of course, to deny the existence of a linkage between the state and the dominant class, merely to suggest that the short-term interests of the bourgeoisie and that of the state might conflict in view of the former's preoccupation with profit maximization and the latter's goal of system survival: in the longer term, both had an identical interest in ensuring capitalist dominance and, whatever the extent to which the state delayed the onset of proletarian revolution, this would ultimately take place.

The other major revision of Marx was to adapt his analysis of class relations in the urban, industrial context to those in rural, predominantly agrarian societies. Clearly, if Marx was seen as insisting upon communist revolution as the outcome of progressive stages of development and necessarily preceded by that of capitalism, any extrapolation of his analysis of capitalism to agrarian societies could be regarded as illegitimate: agrarian society was the stage before capitalism, not communism. If, on the other hand, it was argued that Marx was concerned to analyze only the Western pattern of development, then his model could be utilized to explain other cases, i.e. to substitute landlords and peasants for bourgeoisie and proletarians and point to developments in class relations leading to communist revolution along the same lines as in capitalist society. In this way, Marx's legacy was adapted to explain the great peasant revolutions of the present century: the most noted exponent of this elaboration of Marx was of course Mao Tse-Tung.[40]

These modifications or extensions of Marx's model were obviously derived from attempts to account for the absence of communist revolutions in the capitalist West and their presence in agrarian societies; but, of course, their adoption in this context implied that they might also be relevant in some degree to explain other patterns. Marx's basic model had not predicted the development of fascism; perhaps by allowing for variations in class/state relations and considering class conflict in the agrarian, as well as the industrial context, the growth of fascism could be explained. Further, if it was admitted that the interests of the dominant class and those of the state might diverge in the short term in modern capitalist societies, or that agrarian class relations were more important than had been realized, it was conceivable that the historical importance of these factors had been overlooked. Thus the debate over the apparently poor predictive power of Marx's model stimulated modifications of his theory to explain the resilience of capitalism and the occurrence of peasant communist revolutions, and these in turn generated research to try to explain the occurrence of fascism and to re-analyze historical patterns of change.

BARRINGTON MOORE AND THE SOCIAL ORIGINS OF DICTATORSHIP AND DEMOCRACY

The first major work in which an attempt was made to sustain the basic thrust of some of Marx's ideas[41] while incorporating the amendments noted above was Barrington Moore's *The Social Origins of Dictatorship and Democracy,* published in 1967. Moore defined his objective as the explanation of

> the varied political roles played by the landed upper classes and the peasantry in the transformation from agrarian societies (defined simply as states where a large majority of the population lives off the land) to modern industrial ones. Somewhat more specifically, it is an attempt to discover the range of historical conditions under which either or both of these groups have been important behind the emergence of

Western parliamentary versions of democracy, and dictatorships of the right and left, that is, fascist and communist regimes.[42]

The methodology adopted to examine this was not the hyperthetico-deductive approach usually employed in the social sciences,[43] but that of comparative historical analysis. The former type of methodology involves the specification of a theory to account for a particular phenomenon, the derivation of appropriate hypotheses which are in principle falsifiable, and the testing of these to determine the validity of the initial explanation. The comparative historical method is, by contrast, an inductive approach whereby a range of historical cases relevant to the particular concerns of the research are studied in detail, contrasts between cause and effect mechanisms established by comparison, and explanations derived upon this basis. Thus Moore selected cases to represent each path to the modern world. England, France and the United States were chosen as examples of the bourgeois revolutionary route to parliamentary democracy; the fascist path of 'revolution from above' was catered for by Japan with some additional material on Germany; the case of communist peasant revolution taken was that of China, and this was complemented by some reference to patterns in Russia. Moore also included India among the cases to be analyzed. The reason given for this was that India apparently offered a check upon the findings derived from other cases as it was a society which had seen little modernization, which had a peasantry at least as deprived as those in China and Russia, but which had some of the historical prerequisites of parliamentary democracy.[44] It was considered that any variables used to explain the various revolutionary paths to the modern world could be verified by their ability to account for the absence of one or other revolutionary path in the Indian case. Thus, for example, any set of factors identified which purported to explain why China and Russia experienced peasant communist revolutions could be applied to the Indian case; clearly, if they offered a good fit, this would indicate that additional variables were required to explain the difference in outcomes between the former and the latter patterns of development.

Skocpol[45] has suggested that Moore analyzed his case studies with reference to three main variables. The first was the strength of the bourgeois impulse in particular societies. Marx had advanced the proposition that, in feudal societies, the interests of industrial and commercial capitalists would ultimately clash with those of the dominant landowning classes and increasing confrontation would lead to a revolution in which the former would overthrow the latter. Moore modified this in two ways. He stressed the role of agrarian capitalism – the growth of landowning groups, sometimes from within the traditional landed classes, who farmed for profit – and he allowed for variations in the strength of the impetus towards the creation of a capitalist society, this depending upon the extent to which mass cultural values were favourable or unfavourable to modernization. The second variable deployed by Moore was the form of commercial agriculture. This was divided into the 'labour-repressive' form, in which the landowning classes directly exploited the peasantry, and the 'market' variant, whereby the agricultural system involved a labour-market within which capitalists hired and fired wage labourers. The latter, of course, were the rural equivalent of Marx's urban proletariat. The final variable identified by Skocpol was the revolutionary potential of the peasantry. Just as Marx[46] had pointed up the different patterns of relations between classes in the small craft workshops and the large mass-production unit, Moore noted that the revolutionary potential of the peasantry was lower where there were strong paternalistic bonds between the latter and landlords than where ties were weak and relations overtly exploitative. Skocpol's schema did not include one additional variable used by Moore (although it was mentioned in her account), which was the relationship between the state and the various classes in society. Moore departed from Marxist orthodoxy, and allowed for degrees of relative dependence or independence of the state from the ruling class. Overall, Moore's analysis was thus an extension of Marx's constructs into the realm of agrarian class relations, but with the introduction of cultural variables (explaining the strength of the bourgeois impulse) and a different perspective on class–state relations.

The case studies indicated that different configurations of these variables were associated with different outcomes in terms of social change. From the standpoint of the study of revolution, it is perhaps most helpful to start with Moore's analysis of his 'control' case, India, the only one of those selected which did not have a revolution: clearly the difference between this and other cases illuminates Moore's answer to the question as to the patterns promoting revolution or non-revolution. Moore argued that, with respect to strength of bourgeois impulse, there were very considerable obstacles to modernization in India. Prior to the British conquest, India was an 'oriental despotism',[47] where Mogul rule was absolute and unthreatened by aristocratic or bourgeois privileges or liberties, i.e. the political system was such that new groups which might challenge the regime could be destroyed before they became effective. This very rigidity, however, proved the downfall of the Mogul empire; in the absence of an impulse towards modernization, the system remained static and eventually simply broke down, thus opening the door to European conquest in the eighteenth century. The conquerors, the British, of course tried to modernize India, but were unable to do so successfully because (1) they sent the profits of imperialism home rather than investing in industrial growth and (2) they incurred the active hostility of the population to modernization as this became identified with the imposition of a Western 'scientific' culture upon existing norms and values. Modernization thus became an unacceptable component of imperialism, and the maintenance of a traditional society part of the ideology of nationalism. This association, Moore suggested, continued into post-independence India, where the impulse towards modernization remained relatively weak. With regard to the other variables, Moore noted that agriculture was labour-repressive, to an extent which was greater than in China or Japan; but the revolutionary potential of the peasantry was low because of the caste system, which provided a rigid basis of religiously-sanctified stratification, with appropriate norms and values for each caste. Rebellion or revolution was not, in this context, an attempt to remodel secular structures but a total challenge to a religiously-sanctified and deeply engrained social structure. The state, Moore claimed, was (at least in the case of the period of British rule) tied to the upper landed classes and their interests. This was significant, in that the British alienated the bourgeoisie by their policy of not investing surpluses in India and this class proved unwilling to join with the landed classes to modernize 'from above'. A final product of the association between the British and the upper landed classes was that the influence of the former was important in instilling the cultural values appropriate to parliamentary democracy among the latter, and thus contributing to the adoption and maintenance of such a political system. It may be noted that Moore was not optimistic as to the ability of a democratic system in India to modernize the country, particularly as this was still associated with undesirable Western influences.

Those countries with historical experiences closest to India in Moore's schema were Russia and China, which had had peasant communist revolutions. In both of these cases the 'bourgeois impulse' was comparatively weak;[48] agriculture was labour-repressive; and the state was associated with a landed upper class and weakened in authority as a consequence of inability to modernize.[49] However, Moore pointed out that both China and Russia had a long history of peasant revolts and rebellions prior to their respective revolutions.[50] The apparent failure in these two countries to integrate large sections of the peasantry reflected rather different factors. In the Chinese case, peasant radicalism stemmed from relationships between landlord and peasant which resembled those in a totalitarian political system.[51] The landlord was an effective dictator who governed by direct and repressive methods. The effect of this was the creation of a dissatisfied peasantry which was unable to combine in normal circumstances to oppose the landlords because of the nature of the repression to which it was subject (police surveillance was used by landlords to keep informed as to the emergence of group oppositions which were then ruthlessly destroyed in their infancy). The Chinese peasantry was thus a potentially radical, but largely unstructured, mass, which was periodically exploited beyond acceptable levels and reacted in large-scale, generally disorganized, rebellion. The Communist party was able to tap this tradition, and succeed where other movements had failed in providing structures to create longer-term solidarity and make a revolution. The peasants in Russia, by way of contrast, had a high revolutionary potential for other reasons: they were noted for their solidarity as groups in disputes with their overlords, a factor which Moore explained partly in terms of the historical tradition of village solidarity, and partly in terms of the impact of reforms in the late nineteenth and early twentieth centuries which provided for land redistribution and united the rich peasants (upset by the prospect of losing land) and the poorer ones (whose expectations as to redistribution were almost bound to be disappointed).[52] The Bolsheviks in Russia had thus both a radical peasantry and an organizational basis for mobilizing them to revolt.

In the two cases where modernization led to fascist revolution, Germany and Japan, the peasantry had a low level of revolutionary potential, agriculture was labour-repressive, and there were unique configurations of the state and the landed classes vis-à-vis a moderately-strong bourgeoisie.[53] In both of these countries there was some industrialization during the late nineteenth and early twentieth centuries, which led to the growth of a weak industrial bourgeoisie; in addition, there was the development of a landlord class which engaged in commercial agriculture but needed to change existing patterns of land tenure and working (and in consequence the rural social structure) in order to increase profits; finally there was a state bureaucracy allied to the landlord class and committed to modernization. Moore argued that these three groups combined to bring about revolution from above, fascism, and destroy traditional peasant society in the interests of creating a capitalist economy. Moore noted[54] that the amount of destruction necessary varied; in Japan there was fairly minimal tinkering (enough to enable the agrarian bourgeoisie to 'farm' by expropriating feudal dues), whereas in other countries the process went considerably further. He explained the repression associated with fascism in terms of dealing with peasant opposition to modernization, and the need to create quickly a disciplined, skilled labour force.

The final classification of revolutions used by Moore was that of 'bourgeois' revolutions leading to parliamentary democracy. These cases – England, France and the United States – shared one characteristic to themselves, that of a comparatively strong 'bourgeois impulse' at an early stage of the modernization process. The bourgeois class was strongest in England, and an alliance of commercially-oriented gentry and urban commercial interests were able to defeat the traditional aristocracy in the English revolution, and later impose industrialization;[55] in the United States a Northern urban bourgeoisie defeated a Southern landed elite in the Civil War;[56] in France an agrarian bourgeoisie which was capitalist by virtue of extracting feudal dues from the peasantry for profit overthrew the remnants of a feudal regime to create a capitalist society.[57] Beyond this factor, these various countries shared little. England and the United States, in so far as they had a peasant class at all, had a peasantry with a low potential for revolution; in France there was a large peasant mass, which, as it was directly exploited by both aristocracy and the agrarian bourgeoisie, had a high revolutionary potential.[58] France was again unique in that it had a predominantly 'labour-repressive' agricultural system; in England and the United States agriculture was organized on a market basis. Finally, with regard to state–class relations, the state appears to have been relatively independent of the various classes within English society;[59] in France the state became an appendage of the aristocracy during the late eighteenth century;[60] in the United States one of the central issues over which the Civil War was fought was as to which class the state should favour,[61] which would suggest that prior to the Civil War the state could not be identified completely with either class. It is apparent that the factors which were responsible for the 'bourgeois democratic' path to modernization differed between the cases studied by Moore.

The findings of the analysis of the various case studies are summarized in Figure 1.2. The non-revolutionary case, India, was distinguished from the others by a unique combination of low peasant revolutionary potential and a weak bourgeois impulse; the difference between this outcome and that of peasant communist revolution as in China and Russia was that in the latter the peasants were a revolutionary force; the comparable variation between India and Japan and Germany was that the strength of the bourgeois impulse in the two countries which had undergone fascist revolutions was somewhat greater; France, in contrast to India, exhibited both a high potential for revolution among the peasantry and a strong bourgeois impulse, and the outcome of a bourgeois revolution leading to parliamentary democracy apparently illustrates the importance of strength of bourgeois impulse (for France corresponded in other respects to China and Russia which had peasant communist revolutions); England and the United States were qualitatively different from the other cases with market-based agriculture and a high degree of independence between the state and the dominant class: but these features, in conjunction with a low potential for revolution among the peasantry, did not seem to be critical compared to strength of bourgeois impulse given that this was all that they shared with France, the other case of bourgeois revolution. At a general level, Moore's analysis thus suggested that: (1) the necessary and sufficient condition for non-revolution was a conjunction of a conservative peasantry and a weak bourgeois impulse; (2) violation of this by the existence of a radical peasantry would lead to peasant communist revolution; (3) violation by a moderate bourgeois impulse was associated with an outcome in terms of fascist revolution; and (4) a strong bourgeois impulse dominated over other combinations of factors to yield bourgeois revolutions.

Outcome	Cases	System of agriculture	State/class relationship	Peasant revolutionary potential	Strength of bourgeois impulse
Non-revolution	India	Labour-repressive	Dependent	Low	Weak
Peasant communist revolution	China, Russia	Labour-repressive	Dependent	High	Weak
Fascist revolution	Germany, Japan	Labour-repressive	Dependent	Low	Moderate
Bourgeois revolution	France, England, US	Labour-repressive Market	Dependent Independent	High Low	Strong Strong

FIGURE 1.2 *Moore's case-study analysis*

Moore's analysis has been subjected to criticism on the grounds of the validity of the interpretation of the case studies chosen, the choice of case studies, and the inferences drawn from these. Most of the historical scrutiny of the case studies has been of the three countries which were held to have followed the 'bourgeois democratic' path to the modern world. In particular it has been questioned as to whether these had 'bourgeois' revolutions. In the English case, doubts have been expressed as to whether it is correct to describe the Civil War as representing violent conflict between the aristocracy and a modernizing coalition of urban and rural capitalists; more recent research has been quoted[62] to the effect that such an interpretation was not consistent with the pattern of alliances between these groups and the two sides which fought the war. Further, questions have been raised as to whether the outcome of the conflict was the institution of a qualitatively different kind of society, whether the England of 1660 was very much different from the England of 1640. It has been suggested that the main difference was simply that a king had been judicially murdered, which as Rothman[63] noted was neither a unique event nor did it have the social and economic ramifications associated with the modern concept of revolution. Although the word revolution was used by contemporaries to describe the Civil War, it was in the original sense of a return to a starting point, as was noted on p. 1. Similar criticisms may be made of Moore's analysis of the French Revolution. Cobban,[64] in a celebrated attempt to rebut Marxist and neo-Marxist analyses of the French Revolution, questioned the extent to which a 'bourgeois' class with common interests could be identified in pre-revolutionary France, whether it was correct to suggest that the revolution was made by such a class, and whether the outcome of the revolution could be meaningfully described in terms of the institution of a bourgeois society. Doubts may also be expressed as to the description of the American Civil War contained in Moore's analysis; there was no necessary incompatibility between Northern urban-based capitalism and the plantation system based on slavery in the South in economic terms, i.e. it was not apparently a precondition of modernization that the latter was eliminated. Indeed, the relative stability of the plantation system following the American Civil War in the South coupled with industrial growth would appear to support this contention.

The case studies in fascist revolution, Germany and Japan, have likewise attracted criticism. With the former, it has been questioned as to how far there was a revolution at all.[65] Additionally, in view of the mass support for the Nazis, it can be suggested that, if there was a strong modernizing elite, it was not imposing its ideas upon an entirely unwilling population. Japan, as Skocpol[66] suggested, appeared prima facie to offer a better 'fit' to the model in that a substantive modernization programme was carried out with considerable popular opposition. However, the point has been made that this was not a simple case of a state/aristocracy/bourgeois elite coalition modernizing regardless of mass preferences, as advanced by Moore. A number of commentators[67] have claimed that modernization was imposed by a bureaucracy with substantial independence from other groups in society, which was not afraid to attack interests (including those of landlords and capitalists) which it was felt were inimical to Japanese development.

Moore's analysis of China and Russia has received relatively little attention, but his account of the Indian development pattern has been subjected to more detailed scrutiny by Rothman.[68] He suggested that Moore's account of the weakness of the thrust to modernization was misleading, and that account needed to be taken of the inadequate resource base for development as well as the absence, until comparatively recently, of a strong nation state which could direct resources. Bearing these considerations in mind, the lack of a revolution in India compared to the other countries taken could be accounted for in other ways than those used by Moore; further, the period of British rule may be regarded as a positive factor contributing to development rather than an impediment in so far as the British unified the nation and created a central state which could then implement modernization.

This argument is consistent with a general point concerning Moore's work, that he tended to focus exclusively on the determinants and nature of class relations within a society while analyzing modernization, and that this inhibited the explanatory value of his work. By concentrating upon such factors, Moore excluded other variables which might have been important. Thus Moore under-stressed the role of religion in the English Revolution, the place of moral opposition to slavery in the American Civil War, the imperialist ambitions to the bureaucracy in the adoption of a fascist path to modernity in Japan, or the lack of national unification in the Indian case. It is of course a common criticism of Marxist or neo-Marxist models that the use of only one set of variables (or suggesting that others can effectively be subsumed under them as simply ideological manifestations of class interests) reduces the explanatory power of accounts based upon them.

A further point relating to what Moore did not include in his work rather than what he did concerns the number and choice of case studies. It can be argued that, even if there was substantial agreement as to the validity of Moore's analysis of the cases taken, this would constitute but a small sample of the population of countries which have modernized, and thus be subject to sampling error. On the other hand, it is remarkable for one author to have covered as many countries as Moore did, and it could be said that it was then open to others to exploit the legacy of Moore by testing his model with other cases. A more insidious charge is that the selection of cases was deliberately biased in order to influence the results. The use of India (where modernization had been weak and not notably successful) rather than for example the Scandinavian countries (where full modernization has taken place) to illustrate the case of non-revolutionary development has been cited as evidence of Moore's determination to show that a transition to a fully developed society could only be achieved through violent revolution, preferably of a communist kind.[69] In fairness to Moore, it ought to be said that he did comment upon the exclusion of these countries in his introduction, and offered the explanation that the modernization process in them was mainly influenced by external, rather than internal, factors which lay outside the scope of his book.[70] This defence, however, seems somewhat at odds with the inclusion of India as a case study, given the central role played by the British in that country's history; further, if external factors were important, the absence of consideration of these in other case studies may be taken as a criticism of the comprehensiveness of Moore's account.

Overall, the critics of Moore have suggested that the conclusions of the *Social Origins* were dependent upon highly selective interpretations of a biased set of case studies. Thus the analysis of the determinants of non-revolution or revolution reflected a particular view of an atypical case study, that of India; the discussion of types of revolutionary development was marred by questionable assumptions as to whether revolutions had occurred, the uncritical application of class conflict theories, and a neglect of other influences upon social change. On the other hand it can be argued that Moore's work was important in ensuring that the legacy of Marx was not forgotten by social scientists studying revolutions, that it was a pioneering analysis, and as such offered a base upon which others could build. The work of Skocpol in particular can be seen as an attempt to maintain much of the framework developed by Moore from his reassessment of Marx while responding to the various critiques of the *Social Origins*.

SKOCPOL, STATES AND SOCIAL REVOLUTIONS

Moore, as has been seen, allowed for a relative autonomy in relationships between dominant classes and states in his model (although the degree of dependence or independence between these appeared to matter little in determining paths of modernization); Skocpol took this a stage further by granting that states could, at least in principle, be autonomous from dominant classes. This was apparent in her discussion of the focus of her book, the explanation of social revolutions. Skocpol[71] made a distinction between: rebellions, which involved revolts by subordinate classes which were not associated with the social transformation of societies; political revolutions, in which the state was transformed but not the social structures of societies; modernizing revolutions whereby social structures were altered fundamentally but without political upheaval; and social revolutions in which there was a coincidence of lower-class revolt and the transformation of both the social structure and the state. The difference between modernizing and social revolutions indicated that Skocpol did not consider that modernization necessarily required political revolution, i.e. that the role of the state in the modernization process could vary from promoting modernization in the face of opposition from the dominant class through to being overthrown along with that class if modernization was opposed.

Skocpol's book was concerned to (1) explain why some societies modernized through social revolutions, defined as 'rapid, basic transformations of a society's state and class structures . . . accompanied and in part carried through by class-based revolts from below',[72] whereas others did not, and (2) to account for variations between the outcomes of social revolutions. The study was, like that of Moore, based upon the comparative historical analysis of case studies. Those chosen from the set of social revolutions were France, Russia and China. The reasons for choosing these were that: (a) the social revolutions took place in countries whose state and class structures were unaffected by colonialism, which simplified the analysis; (b) they shared similar features prior to the occurrence of social revolutions, including that they were wealthy and politically-ambitious agrarian states with proto-bureaucratic autocracies; (c) patterns of the demise of Old Regimes were similar, particularly in that they involved a conjuncture of political crisis and widespread peasant revolts; (d) following the replacement of the Old Regimes, there were attempts to mobilize the masses to consolidate revolutionary power and outcomes in terms of the creation of centralized, bureaucratic and mass-mobilizing nation states with enhanced power in the international arena; (e) but there were variations in the types of social and political transformations; and (f) the social revolutions had occurred long enough in the past to permit the study of the revolutionary process as a whole. Reasons (a)–(d) implied that France, China and Russia could be treated as a common set of cases with respect to the occurrence of social revolutions as opposed to other types of revolutions, and explained in terms of a common set of variables. In order to evaluate these negatively, i.e. establish that variables identified as applying to these cases also distinguished them from others, Skocpol also studied a number of cases where modernization had taken place without social revolutions. These included variously Russia in 1905, the Meiji restoration in Japan, Prussia/Germany in the first half of the nineteenth century, and the English Civil War. The last two reasons cited, (e) and (f) above, related to the second objective of the study, the analysis of differences in the patterns of revolutionary transformations. France, Russia and China offered a spread of types – in France the creation of a modern state edifice, in Russia the emergence of a dictatorial party state and in China the development of a mass-mobilizing party state – to explain, and enough historical distance from the completion of transformations to allow meaningful analysis.

With regard to the causes of social, as distinct from other kinds, of revolutions, the logic of both the definition of social revolutions and reason (c) given for the choice of case studies dictated a focus upon those factors determining the coincidence of political crisis and revolts from below, the coincidence which distinguished the class of social revolutions from non-social revolutions. Skocpol[73] asserted that this could only be analyzed in terms of structural variables, and their dynamic interrelationships over time; she eschewed the notion that social revolutions were explicable in non-structural terms, for example the success of a revolutionary movement in spreading its ideology among the masses, and rejected the implication of the latter type of explanation that revolutions were 'voluntarist' in character, i.e. that whether or not they occurred depended upon the success or otherwise of state or revolutionary actors in mobilizing support. Social revolutions could only be explained by identifying the set of determining structural factors: they followed inevitably from particular, and predetermined, configurations of such factors.

The various case studies were analyzed by reference to five sets of variables which might have explained the conjunction of crisis and revolt promoting social revolution (or the absence of this and hence modernization by other means). Skocpol took firstly the determinants of the various forms of internal socio-economic structures. Under this heading she included the nature of production in agrarian systems, whether this was pre-capitalist or in transition to agrarian capitalism. The mode of production was held to determine the nature of classes, and class relations, and hence the environment within which modernization took place. Secondly, Skocpol tried to identify whether, among the traditional agrarian systems, production was so organized as to yield a surplus to pay for modernization, or whether the generation of such a surplus required the expropriation of resources from landlords and/or peasants. The third group of factors related to the nature of the state and its relationship with the upper landed classes in society: the former concerned whether there was a large bureaucratic or semi-bureaucratic state, the latter the extent to which the state was controlled and influenced by a politically-powerful landed class. Skocpol then introduced variables relating to location within the international economic system, in particular the extent to which countries were subject to extreme, strong, moderate or mild military pressures from capitalist countries seeking to expand their markets. Finally, she noted that there were 'historically specific institutional arrangements'[74] which related to the revolutionary potential of the peasantry. These included (1) whether agriculture was of a large estate kind (where serfs and labourers were directly exploited by landlords and their agents, kept poor and disciplined, which restricted revolutionary potential) or of a rentier-agrarian type (where smallholders owned and worked the land independently with a surplus being extracted indirectly, which encouraged combination in defence of common interests and increased revolutionary potential); and (2) whether control over peasants was exerted locally by landlords (in which case any basis for united action could be identified, controlled, destroyed or diverted) or by a remote central bureaucracy (where responses to mobilization were likely to be slower and less effective). Skocpol thus sought explanations of the occurrence or non-occurrence of social revolutions in terms of the application of Marx's work in the context of agrarian structures and the international environment; but this was coupled with a denial of at least the orthodox Marxist interpretation of necessary dependency between the state and the upper landed classes, and the use of structural–political, rather than structural–economic, variables to analyze the revolutionary potential of the peasantry. The dynamic interrelationships between these variables were revealed in the course of comparison of the various case studies.

Pre-revolutionary France[75] was a traditional, pre-capitalist agrarian society, with the appropriate class structure, namely a dominant landed upper class which expropriated surpluses from the peasantry. The dominant class was partly dependent upon, and had considerable influence within, a semi-bureaucratic absolute monarchical state. This had imperialist pretensions, as manifested by support for the Americans in their War of Independence, and was contending militarily with capitalist England to modernize and to play a major role in the world system. However, the traditional agricultural system failed to generate an adequate surplus to pay for war and internal development, and the state became bankrupt; in order to sustain its ambitions, it was forced to find new sources of revenue, which involved impinging upon the privileges of the landed upper classes. This threat effectively removed much of the support of the upper landed classes for the state, and precipitated a political crisis. The state's attempt to resolve this by convening the Estates General in 1789 triggered widespread peasant revolts; the Third Estate was effectively asked to list its grievances, and these focused long-standing discontent among a peasantry with a high radical potential reflecting an absence of local control and the fact that agriculture was predominantly of a rentier-agrarian type. The political crisis meant that neither the state nor the dominant landed class had full control of the military, of the means of coercion, and hence the revolts were pushed to a successful conclusion, to the abolition of the Old Regime.

China[76] was similar in many respects to France. There was a dominant class of gentry which held office in the state, and which extracted surpluses from the peasantry within the framework of a traditional agrarian system. These surpluses were being rapidly exhausted by population growth during the nineteenth century; when, in the late nineteenth and early twentieth centuries, the Manchu rulers were pressurized to react to European capitalist expansionism by reforming the structures and institutions of

Chinese society to enable it to cope with the modern world, they had to try and extract the necessary surplus to pay for this from the gentry. This challenged the regime and forced political crisis; in 1911 the Manchu dynasty fell. However, unlike the French case, this was not immediately accompanied by peasant revolt, but by a period of 'warlordism' followed by attempts at national reunification and urban revolts. Skocpol accounted for this failure by claiming that the Chinese peasantry were, by virtue of their structural position (under the direct, and effective, local control of landlords), limited to social banditry as a response to crisis and inequality. It was only when the Chinese Communist party provided the direction and structuration for action that peasant revolts took place.

Russia,[77] in common with France and China, had a pre-capitalist mode of agriculture which was unable to generate a surplus to pay for modernization; but the landed nobility was weak relative to the highly bureaucratic absolutist state, largely in consequence of the reforms of Peter the Great. When, in the late nineteenth and early twentieth centuries, the state tried to modernize Russia in the face of extreme economic and military pressure from the developing European capitalist nations, it did not have to contend with a politically-powerful, recalcitrant landed nobility, but neither could it rely upon this class for support. Rapid industrialization from above destroyed regime support among the peasantry which was expected to pay for modernization, and this generated revolts among a peasantry with a high revolutionary potential by virtue of their experience in uniting a village level to counter direct central control by the bureaucracy; industrialization also displaced many peasants from rural to urban areas, and created new disaffected groups in the latter. Thus the Russian state became isolated from, and opposed by, the major classes in Russian society. As long as it retained control of the means of coercion, the coincidence of peasant revolts and political crisis could be avoided (as in 1905). However, in 1917, the pressures generated by involvement and defeat in war exacerbated political crisis, encouraged urban and peasant revolts and, most critically, deprived the state of the military means of repression, with the consequence of social revolution.

Skocpol then contrasted these cases with others where modernization was accomplished without social revolution. In Japan,[78] the Meiji Restoration (1868–73) was a sudden and fundamental change in the political organization of society (a transformation from regionally-based aristocratic governments to a modern, centralized nation state) which followed strong international pressures from the capitalist West. The Restoration laid the basis for future modernization, but without the upheaval of social revolution. This, Skocpol argued, was in large part made possible by the absence of a landed class with political power at the centre, by the separation between this class and the central state bureaucracy. The latter was autonomous, and able to promote modernization without disintegration consequent upon withdrawal of support by the landed nobility (unlike France and China). Of course this configuration was similar in some respects to that in Russia; but, Skocpol suggested, there were two critical differences between the cases. In Japan, while agriculture was pre-capitalist in structure, there was a surplus available for modernization which could be financed without significant hardship to the peasantry or the introduction of foreign capital. This avoided state-led modernization alienating key groups and causing political crisis. In addition, the external pressures to modernize in Japan, while strong, were weaker than those on Russia, the latter competing to be a major capitalist power within the most developed capitalist arena in the world, the former with more limited objectives within a less developed region.

Skocpol also discussed modernization in Prussia/Germany[79] during the early and mid-nineteenth century. In Prussia a variety of reforms were initiated between 1807 and 1814; there was a failed social revolution in Germany in 1848. She argued that these reflected a similar phenomenon to Japan, with the bureaucratic state divorced from the landed upper class at national level, and thus able to modernize without losing its main prop in society; unlike Russia this took place within an economic system where agriculture was in transition to agrarian capitalism to which both landed classes and peasants had adapted, and where there was a surplus available to finance modernization. The revolutionary potential of the peasantry varied between different regions: those west of the Elbe had a relatively high potential, as they lived in autonomous villages ruled remotely; those to the east were under local junker control and working in a large estate milieu, which inhibited the development of structured communities which could provide a basis for political action. The early modernization in

Prussia was forced by strong international pressures but, given that neither the landed classes nor the peasantry were unduly squeezed to finance it, the state was able to avoid alienating key groups; milder international pressures in 1848 promoted minor political crisis, but this was not accompanied by a total revolt of the peasantry. Those west of the Elbe revolted, but they were not followed by those east of the Elbe, which enabled the state to concentrate its forces upon the former and retain control.

The final negative case was the English Civil War,[80] which Skocpol viewed as an example of modernization with political, rather than social, revolution. England differed from the other cases in that there was no massive bureaucratic state: the upper landed classes governed. The impetus to modernization came not from the state, but from that section of the upper landed class engaged in capitalist agriculture and commerce. This class, under mild international pressures, had secured economic dominance prior to the Civil War, i.e. the traditional agricultural system had generated a surplus adequate to pay for modernization, and England was in transition to agrarian capitalism. This had been accomplished without alienating the peasantry, which was in any case small in numbers and limited in revolutionary potential by virtue of a combination of localized landlord control and large-estate agriculture. Thus economic and social transformation had to a large extent preceded the Civil War: the latter was a political revolution in which the agrarian capitalist wing of the upper landed classes had added political to economic dominance by enforcing rule by a parliament under its control.

Skocpol's findings are summarized schematically in Figure 1.3. It is apparent that the cause of the fundamental political crises in the cases of social revolutions was (1) the attempt of state bureaucracies to respond to international pressures by modernizing when (2) the surplus generated by pre-capitalist agrarian systems was inadequate to finance this except by attacking the privileges of politically-powerful upper landed classes (France and China) or non-powerful upper landed classes and the peasantry (Russia) which (3) was responsible for the disintegration of traditional sources of support for the state and the loss of its monopoly of the means of coercion. In each of the societies where this occurred, institutional arrangements were such as to promote a high revolutionary potential among the peasantry which revolted. The state, without control of the military, was unable to repress these and was swept overboard in a tide of revolution.

Case	Domestic agriculture		State and class		International dimension	Peasantry	
	Surplus to finance modernization	Type of agricultural system	Bureaucratic size	Politically-powerful landed class	International competitive/ military pressures	Peasant revolutionary potential	Outcome
Germany 1848	Yes	In transition	Yes	Yes	Mild	Low	Failed social revolution
Prussia 1806–14					Strong	Low	Modernizing revolution
English Civil War			No	Yes	Mild	Low	Political revolution
Meiji Restoration in Japan		Pre-capitalist	Yes	No	Strong	Low	Modernizing revolution
France	No	Pre-capitalist	Yes	Yes	Moderate	High	Social revolution
China				Yes	Strong	High	Social revolution
Russia				No	Extreme	High	Social revolution

FIGURE 1.3 *Skocpol's analysis of revolutions*

The cases of modernization without social revolution shared two common features. Firstly, there was a surplus available for modernization, whether this was generated in a traditional agrarian system (Japan) or one in transition to agrarian capitalism (Prussia/Germany and England). This meant that modernization could be undertaken by the state without alienating key classes (Japan or Prussia/Germany); in England the capitalist wing of the upper landed classes was able to modernize the economic system without unduly penalizing traditional landowners, which restricted conflict to the political arena. For these reasons, the extent of crisis consequent upon modernization was limited and, critically, did not extend as far as the state's loss of control over the means of coercion (in Japan and Prussia/Germany): the latter meant that peasant revolts could be contained (as in 1848 when the peasants west of the Elbe revolted). The second factor was that, in general, institutional structures were such as to inhibit widespread peasant revolts (which were absent in Japan and Prussia and did not occur among peasants east of the Elbe in 1848). These factors prevented the emergence of the conjunction of fundamental crisis and large-scale peasant revolts which characterized social revolutions.

The vast majority of theorists of revolution have remained content to explain the demise of Old Regimes, a focus which stemmed from a definition of revolution in terms of political change rather than other criteria. Skocpol's class of social revolutions, however, stretched the definition of revolution to include social transformation, and the second part of her book was devoted to the analysis of the source and nature of variations in this component of the revolutionary process. The focus of Skocpol's analysis was upon state-building,[81] upon the way in which a new state was constructed following the initial phase of the revolution. The direction of attention to this particular aspect was explained in that state-building was itself an important part of a revolutionary transformation, and that the process of state-building constrained and influenced the ways in which social transformations were influenced. Skocpol outlined three categories of variables which dictated the nature of the process of state-building, namely the nature of social revolutionary crises, the socio-economic legacy of the Old Regime, and international circumstances. As with the discussion of the origins of social revolutionary crises, she insisted that these were structural in character, and outcomes reflected inevitable results of structural interactions: she specifically denied that the nature of revolutionary movements seizing power, especially their ideologies, were important determinants of types of social transformations, a contention which was of course in accord with her downgrading of revolutionary parties as causal variables in explaining the fall of Old Regimes.

Skocpol identified various common elements determining the processes of state-building in France, Russia and China.[82] In all of these cases: (1) social revolutionary crises weakened the hold of dominant classes and this, in conjunction with persisting peasant revolts, made liberalization (in the sense of an English-type parliamentary system dominated by a section of the upper landed class) ultimately impossible; (2) the Old Regime legacy of a predominantly agrarian system with a significant, and disaffected, peasantry meant that any stable new regime had to incorporate this group; (3) involvement in competition in the international economic system and imperialist or defensive wars dictated the creation of a state with the capability to ensure success. Thus the process of state-building involved the sweeping away of the privileges of landed classes in the interests of the politico-military mobilization of popular support for a domestically- and internationally-powerful nation state: the outcome was a qualitatively-different kind of society from that of the Old Regime, and a state which was larger, more bureaucratic and more mass-incorporating than its predecessor.

There were of course variations as well as similarities in the factors determining the process of state-building and social transformations. In France, the social revolutionary crisis and peasant revolts swept away what Skocpol, quoting Marx, termed the 'medieval rubbish'[83] of the Old Regime – seigneural rights, local privileges, municipal and guild monopolies and provincial constitutions – but left the distribution of landed property virtually unchanged. France remained a predominantly agrarian country, without an industrial base for new regimes to capitalize upon: in any case Skocpol suggested that state-led industrialization was not yet a 'world-historical possibility'.[84] In the international context, France became involved in continental military competition to become a major power following the initial phase of revolution. The process of revolutionary state-building in France was at first the mobilization of military support, a task undertaken by the Jacobin proto-party; while this succeeded in consolidating the military, it did not acquire a base in industry (there was no urban proletariat) nor within the peasantry (which was not bonded to the Jacobins for gains in the same way as, for example, the Chinese peasantry was beholden to the Communist party for land redistribution). In consequence, the Jacobins fell following military reorganization and the latter came to power in the Napoleonic military dictatorship. This had the task of rebuilding the administrative structures of the state, a task which, Skocpol suggested, involved the creation of the social and political structures appropriate to the later development of a capitalist economic system. This particular form of the state was the best available to enable France to eventually compete effectively in the international capitalist world order. It may be noted that this argument effectively stood Marx on his head; far from changes in the economic system determining changes in the political, social and legal superstructure, Skocpol argued that in France the latter were changed prior to the former, i.e. that economic change was consequent upon political change. This claim enabled her to argue that France had a social revolution without contending that France had a bourgeois revolution in Marx's sense of the phrase and being subjected to criticism similar to that made of Moore's analysis of the French case (see p. 32).

There were marked differences between the determinants of state-building described above and those in Russia. In the latter, the effects of crisis and peasant revolt were massive changes in which the peasantry drove out the landlords, redistributed property, and then organized within villages to protect their gains. The legacy of the old regime was an agrarian system, but with a considerable development of industry in the key urban areas. Internationally, Russia was under attack from the capitalist West, both militarily and industrially. State-building took the following form: the Bolshevik party had its roots in the urban proletariat, with no support among the peasantry and, in order to survive internal and external attack, was forced to rebuild the state as a coercive apparatus which could repress opposition and force collectivization of the peasantry to generate a surplus to pay for rapid industrialization. The end product was a hierarchical, authoritarian, coercive party state which controlled national economic development; to advance the latter, it countenanced very considerable inequalities of status and economic rewards.

The final pattern was that manifest in China. There the effects of social revolutionary crisis were, as was noted on p. 39, a period of warlordism and of social banditry among the peasantry. The legacy of the Old Regime was a traditional agrarian system, leavened only slightly by industrial development. The international environment was one of defence against external attack during the Second World War, and a hostile environment dominated by the USSR and the United States in the early postwar period. The course of state-building was that the Chinese Communist party, following unsuccessful attempts to promote urban insurrection, mobilized the peasantry and encouraged restructuring by land redistribution. The outcome was a party state, but one decentralized to a considerable extent and with a mass base among the peasantry; the state promoted industrialization, but retained a strong emphasis upon agricultural and rural development, while sustaining the egalitarianism promoted prior to the ending of the revolution.

Skocpol completed her book with a consideration of how far her analysis of the origins and nature of social revolutions could be generalized beyond the particular cases chosen for study.[85] She suggested that the *detailed* causal arguments derived from the French, Chinese and Russian cases could not simply be extended to other social revolutions, for example those in Mexico, Yugoslavia, Vietnam, Algeria, Cuba, Bolivia, Angola, Mozambique, Guinea-Bissau and Ethiopia. While there were some similarities between these cases and those she studied – all were predominantly agrarian countries, revolutions were made possible by the breakdown of the state and peasant revolts, outcomes were strengthened states which consolidated revolutionary changes and asserted national autonomy – there were differences in social structures and state organizations (reflecting variously colonialism and developments among militaries) as well as in the international environment (in particular the effect of competition between the superpowers to gain support among Third World nations). While these variations inhibited the application of specific findings to other cases, Skocpol asserted that her general approach could be adapted to offer a key to the understanding of modern social revolutions; these should be analyzed by using a structuralist, non-voluntarist perspective, by stressing modes of production and consequent class relations to describe domestic structures, by setting these in their international, world-historical context and, perhaps most critically, by focusing upon state organizations in the context of the dynamics of domestic and international structural interactions. Thus Skocpol did not consider her work to be applicable in detail to all revolutions, but has offered a general theory within which these could be analyzed.

States and Social Revolutions was the most comprehensive and ambitious of the 'third wave' studies of revolutions in its explanatory scope and breadth of argument: it was also based in historical and sociological scholarship of a high order. However, it is possible to question various aspects of Skocpol's work, both within its own terms of reference as a structural-determinist model of revolutions and with regard to the general utility of such models in explaining revolutions. Under the former heading, there are queries as to the nature and status of Skocpol's use of the international economy and 'world-historical possibilities' to analyze revolutions. Her recognition of the importance of the international environment as a factor in revolutions was a major (if not unique[86]) contribution: but on occasion the use of this set of variables seemed to be less a matter of illuminating the case studies than maintaining the integrity of the model of social revolutions. Two instances of this may be cited. Firstly, the French Revolution was different from those in China and Russia in terms of its outcome. Skocpol argued that in France the revolution led to changes in political and legal arrangements, but the economic base of society was not transformed until later; in Russia and China these transformations proceeded together. This discrepancy was difficult to explain given the similarities of internal agrarian class structures and state structures between the cases. Skocpol overcame this problem by suggesting that the cause lay in some part in the world-historical possibilities available at particular times in history. Thus – for reasons which remained unexplained – industrialization was not an option open to France while it was a possibility for Russia and China. A second instance was the analysis of China. This differed from France and Russia in so far as the collapse of the Old Regime was not immediately followed by peasant revolt. This was explained in terms of differences in the structural situation of the Chinese peasantry compared to that in France and Russia. Skocpol then had to explain why, some two decades after the fall of the Manchu dynasty, the Chinese peasantry did revolt. At this point she brought in developments in the world situation which forced the Chinese Communist party to adopt a particular strategy of politico-military mobilization which created counter-structures to those pertaining and facilitated revolutionary activity among the peasantry. In both of these cases, the intervention of international forces was used by Skocpol to account for variations which could not be inferred from the other variables in the model. This would not be critical if Skocpol had provided an analysis of the working of the international system which could be used to independently predict why and how such forces should intervene at particular points in the revolutionary process, but such a specification was lacking. This generates at least a suspicion that the international system was not a genuine independent variable, but a means of enabling the *ad hoc* introduction of explanations to rectify deficiencies in the predictive power of other variables.

Skocpol's use of a structural-determinist model appeared to be based upon preference[87] and that she had shown that social revolutions could be explained without recourse to non-structural variables.[88] These grounds were not sufficient in themselves to prove the case: it is possible to argue that (1) there were non-structural variables which were important in explaining revolutions and (2) any relationship between structural variables and revolutionary outcomes was mediated by non-structural factors. With respect to the first point, most of the other theorists whose work is discussed in this book offer non-structural variables as causes of revolution, and demonstrate that these can be 'fitted' to particular cases, including some of those studied by Skocpol. Thus there is no primafacie reason to reject the use of such variables entirely. With regard to the second point, it has been suggested that, while structural variables may provide a framework for action, the relationship between structures and outcomes depends upon the orientations or skills of the actors involved. The general point that there are limits to structural explanations can be illustrated by Lewis's[89] analysis of why there was a mass revolt in Hungary in 1956 but not in Poland. He carefully compared the social, economic and political structures of the two countries but concluded that structural differences were inadequate to explain the incidence of revolt; the latter was related to higher expectations of political autonomy from the USSR among the Hungarians compared to the Poles, and thus greater disappointment and reaction to attempts by the USSR to tighten control over its satellites in 1956. Thus the orientations of the population were the critical explanatory variable, not particular structural configurations.

It is possible to illustrate how an account using non-structural variables might contrast with that presented by Skocpol by taking the case of China. As has been noted, Skocpol provided a structural analysis of non-revolt and then revolt among the peasantry. It could, however, be suggested that this reflected changing perceptions of the likelihood of successful revolt among the Chinese peasantry, a factor identified by the 'economic' theorists of revolutions (see pp. 98–106). The Chinese peasantry was involved in two major rebellions in the mid-nineteenth century, the Taiping Rebellion (1850–65) and the Nien Rebellion (1852–8), both of which had been unsuccessful and costly (the casualties in the Taiping Rebellion have been estimated at twenty million).[90] The peasantry may not have revolted in 1911 because there was a reasonable appreciation that the chances of success were small: it was only when the Communist party mobilized support in the 1940s that the chances of success were raised to a level which made revolutionary activity worthwhile. Another variant of the argument of the economic theorists might have been that the Chinese peasantry had little appreciation of the likely gains from revolution prior to the appearance of the Communist party, which successfully disseminated an ideology which provided adequate incentives to revolt. Skocpol specifically rejected such a role for a revolutionary movement; the tactics and strategy of the Chinese Communist party were dictated by developments in the international system, which determined the way in which support was mobilized, the success of such mobilization, and the presence of a greater mass-mobilizing element in the outcome of the Chinese Revolution than in France or Russia. However, the point may be made that the denial of any latitude for a revolutionary movement to fail or succeed or to mould social revolutions in a particular direction was purely a matter of assumption. It could, for example, be argued following Wolf[91] that the way in which the Chinese Communist party mobilized support during and after the revolution was a consequence of its leaders applying the traditional Confucian doctrine of a non-hereditary, open and meritocratic ruling class in the arena of the relationship between party and masses. Thus this characteristic of the Chinese Revolution could have reflected cultural factors rather than the structural ones which Skocpol assumed to be relevant. Further, even if revolutionary parties like the Chinese Communists were constrained to act as agents of structural change, Skocpol's analysis involved the assumption that they were necessarily able to fulfil this role, i.e. that there was no margin for a revolutionary movement to fail in performing structurally-determined functions. It is, however, at least possible to make the argument that one of the major reasons why the Communist party rather than the Kuomintang successfully mobilized the peasantry was the ability of its leaders to construct an ideology appropriate to peasant aspirations and to provide organizational facilities for incorporating the peasants. Both movements controlled large areas of rural China while they were engaged in fighting the Japanese; but, as Hinton's[92] study of the impact of the Communists and the Kuomingtang upon a village subject at various times to the rule of both makes clear, the former proved more sympathetic to the plight of the peasantry and were more constructive in improving their lot than the latter. Skocpol's assumption that the characteristics of revolutionary movements did not intervene between structural variables and the outcome in China can thus be contested.

If either of these criticisms concerning the status of the international economic system variable or the admissability of non-structural variables is accepted, then Skocpol's contention that social revolutions could only be understood as the inevitable outcome of structurally-determined processes is open to question. This is not to say that her model can be definitively refuted, but that alternative explanations can be advanced which, given the nature of the study of revolutions, are prima facie as plausible as that put forward by Skocpol. Her claims concerning inevitability and the primacy of structural variables could only be fully substantiated if she had developed her model independently of particular cases and then demonstrated its predictive powers (which ran counter to the comparative historical method) or if she had transformed conclusions based upon case studies into hypotheses which could be tested by reference to other causes. It would thus be misleading to regard Skocpol as having discovered the philosopher's stone of revolutions.

CONCLUSION

The sociological theories offered explanations of revolutions at the macro-societal level, but within this there was a diversion between an approach grounded in a functionalist perspective and which stressed the role of social systems, and other approaches which stemmed from a conflict-coercion view and which emphasized the sources and nature of classes and class conflict, class/state relations and, at least in the case of Skocpol, the international economic system. If these two types of approach are compared, it is fair to say that the conflict-coercion approach would appear to at least be easier to operationalize at the level of case studies.

Chalmers Johnson himself was unable to sustain an account of how his model could be applied in the real world and, as was noted, historians have deployed his model in a limited way and then only at the level of the distinction made between longer- and shorter-term causes of revolutions: Barrington Moore and Skocpol both provided extensive historical case studies which yielded insights and demonstrated the workings of the explanatory variables they adopted.

The latter claimed to have derived considerable inspiration from the work of Marx, and the *Social Origins* and *States and Social Revolutions* may be perceived as attempts to amend Marx's work to take into account developments since his death. It can, however, be queried as to how much of Marx's original model was in fact left after Skocpol's and Moore's reworking: the introduction of independent cultural variables (as specified by Moore to explain variations in the strength of the bourgeois impulse although denied by Skocpol), the potential complete autonomy of the state from the dominant class (in Skocpol's account), and finally the assertion that political change could precede change in the economic base of society (as Skocpol argued was the case in the French Revolution) were quite fundamental modifications of the formulation of Marx's work summarized on pp. 21–2. Collectively they reduce Marx's contribution from the provision of an overarching theory to a partial theory, to use McKenzie's[93] distinction, although, as has been seen, neither Moore nor Skocpol were completely successful in developing comprehensive accounts of their own. One reason for this was a neglect of causes of revolution which lay beyond the ambit of sociological theorizing, causes which some analysts of revolutions would suggest included the psychological dimensions of revolutionary behaviour to be discussed in the next chapter.

2 Socio-psychological Theories of Revolutions

The distinguishing characteristic of psychological theories is a focus upon the explanation of attitudes and behaviour in terms of the mental processes of individuals. The usage of such theories in the context of revolutions was relatively limited until the 1960s; the work of Le Bon[1] and Ellwood[2] in the early years of the present century was followed by a few psychodynamic or psychohistorical studies[3] of individual revolutionary activists or leaders, but the potential contribution of psychology was ignored by most of the 'second wave' theorists. However, psychological theories came into favour during the 1960s in the wake of the widespread adoption of 'behaviouralism' as a paradigm for research in political science. Behaviouralism[4] was a collective term for a set of diverse contentions concerning the objectives and methodology of research in political sciences. The most important of these in the present context was that political science should focus upon the political attitudes and behaviours of individuals and, in explaining these, full account should be taken of the perceptions and mental processes of individuals themselves as well as other factors. It was argued that researchers had over-stressed the role of the objective situations of individuals in determining their political attitudes and behaviour and, in consequence, had produced theories which were contradictory and inadequate. Eckstein[5] provided a number of examples of this from the 'second wave' studies of revolutions. Various theorists had investigated the role of social mobility as a factor inducing revolutions, and concluded that the latter were responses to an absence of social mobility, too much downward mobility, too little upward mobility, or too much upward mobility; others had examined the relationship between economic growth and revolutions, and concluded that an absence of growth, too little growth, too slow growth or too rapid growth were all associated with revolutions. The apparent lack of a clear relationship between either of these factors and revolutions was held to indicate the limited utility of such objective variables: Eckstein suggested that all of these explanations might be true, but only because individuals had perceived that the situation, whatever it was, was unacceptable, and this had been translated into revolutionary behaviours by processes operating within their own minds. Thus, in order to produce adequate explanations of revolutions, it was necessary to specify the perceptions of individuals, how these changed over time, and the mechanisms by which such changes were eventually manifested in revolutionary behaviour. This last requirement directed the attention of researchers towards psychological theories which specified the mental processes linking changes in perceptions to changes in behaviour, and a number of attempts were made to derive psychological theories of revolution. These variously drew from two different strands of psychology, one stressing the importance of cognitions, the other the transformation of frustration into aggression. This distinction is retained for purposes of exposition and discussion and the theories have been grouped according to which particular psychological variant was utilized.

COGNITIVE PSYCHOLOGICAL THEORIES OF REVOLUTIONS

The two cognitive psychological theories of revolutions were based primarily in Festinger's[6] 'theory of cognitive dissonance'. This started from the notion of cognitions, defined as 'any knowledge, opinion or belief about the environment, about oneself or about one's behaviour':[7] these were divided into cognitions which were reality-based, those which were definitional and those which were normative. Sets of cognitions could be irrelevant to each other or, if they were related, be consonant or dissonant, i.e. mutually consistent or inconsistent. Dissonance between cognitions was a disturbing state, which led to tension in the minds of individuals and motivated attempts to alleviate this by reducing dissonance and regaining cognitive balance. Modes of dissonance-reduction could include altering cognitions, withdrawing from whatever arena dissonance was associated with, and changing behaviours to attempt to bring reality-based cognitions into consonance with normative or definitional ones. Thus the theory of cognitive dissonance provided linkages between changes in perceptions (which would lead to dissonance by unbalancing cognitions) and behavioural outcomes (which flowed from attempts to reduce psychic tension caused by dissonance) and as such became incorporated in theories of revolutions.

The first theorist who attempted to explain revolutions in terms of cognitive dissonance theory was Geschwender.[8] He conceived of revolutions as involving two components: the first the emergence of a large-scale mass social or protest movement, involving widespread participation in protest activities; the second unspecified 'processes which develop after the protest movement has begun'.[9] Geschwender argued that, in principle, the first component of revolution ought to be explicable in the same terms used generally to analyze social or protest movements; the only difference between the protest movements involved in revolutions and others was in the greater extent of popular participation in protest activities in the former. Given this, he saw his task as the derivation of a general theory which could explain why protest movements emerged and which could also account for differences in the levels of protest activities.

The method adopted by Geschwender to accomplish this was to combine Festinger's theory with others which specified potential sources of cognitive dissonance arising from the development of discrepancies between perceptions or expectations of the past, present or future situations of individuals. Such discrepancies could arise in the following ways: individuals might come to believe that rewards were inadequate relative to educational or ethnic investments or status (the status inconsistency hypothesis); they might anticipate that, given past socio-economic circumstances, a continual improvement in living standards would occur, but then begin to consider that future levels of growth, while positive, would fall short of the expected rate (the rising expectations hypothesis); they might expect continuing growth, and then experience a sudden, and catastrophic, reverse (the rise and drop hypothesis); they might begin to feel that their present situation was significantly worse than it was in the past (the downward mobility hypothesis); or, finally, they might perceive that relevant reference groups would make disproportionate gains in the future compared to their own group (the relative deprivation hypothesis). In each of these cases, discrepancies would lead to dissonance between normative and reality-based cognitions; this would engender psychic tension, and ultimately motivate changes in behaviour to bring the real world into line with expectations and hence achieve cognitive consonance and the consequent reduction or elimination of tension. Such behaviours would be manifested in protest activities, participation in which Geschwender appeared to regard as defining membership of a social or protest movement.

The various hypotheses within this general theory were held to be capable of explaining both the ideological direction of social or protest movements, and the levels of protest activities which occurred. With regard to the former, Geschwender suggested that where comparisons were between the present and the anticipated future (as in the cases of the rising expectations, rise and drop and relative deprivation hypotheses), behaviour would be orientated towards realizing a better state of affairs than had previously existed. Social movements arising from this would be progressive, or 'leftist'; where comparisons were with the past and present, as in the case of downward mobility, behaviour would be designed to restore a previous situation, i.e. would be regressive or 'rightist'. The direction of protest stemming from status inconsistency would vary, depending upon the source of such inconsistency, with those who felt rewards were inadequate to investment in education seeking a change to a meritocracy, while those who sought better rewards for an ethnic investment would look towards the kind of particularistic criteria for reward allocation normally associated with rightist ideologies. With respect to the level of protest, Geschwender assumed that this would be proportional to the intensity of dissonance experienced: the greater the gap between past, actual or expected performances, the greater the dissonance, the higher the level of tension and the more intense the form of dissonance-reducing behaviours. Thus, he argued, the 'rise and drop' pattern would be more likely to produce higher levels of dissonance than the 'rising expectations' one as the level of disparity between expectations and performance was greater. Given this, the resultant behaviours in the former would be more intense than in the latter, and would produce revolutionary rather than reformist social movements. In this way, Geschwender incorporated the explanation of at least part of the revolutionary process within a general theory of the emergence of social or protest movements, these taking a potentially revolutionary form where individuals perceived a large gap between expectations and/or past or present situations, suffered extreme cognitive dissonance in consequence, and adopted intense dissonance-reducing behaviours to alleviate tension. Geschwender noted that this potential might or might not be realized, i.e. that there were other factors which determined whether a revolutionary social movement was successful or unsuccessful in making a revolution, but regarded this as determined by variables other than those specified in his model. He concluded his account by suggesting that, if a social or protest movement failed to achieve change, individuals would respond by altering their cognitions (changing normative cognitions in line with real-world ones) or adopting new cognitions (in particular the futility of attempting to change the system). The latter, he argued, would produce the apathetic, disinterested, non-protest fatalistic behaviours which had been found to be characteristic of the downtrodden.

The second theory of revolutions which stressed the cognitive dimension was that of Schwartz.[10] He defined complete revolution as a set of multi-stage processes, namely (1) initial political alienation (2) the origination of revolutionary organizations (3) revolutionary appeals (4) revolutionary coalition and movement building (5) non-violent revolutionary politics (6) the outbreak of revolutionary violence (7) the rule of a new elite of moderates (8) the accession of the extremists (9) the reign of terror and (10) the return to normality, named Thermidor after the month in the French revolutionary calendar in which Robespierre fell from power and following which internal stability returned under the Directory and then Napoleon. The first six stages were concerned to describe revolutions up to the point at which large-scale violence precipitated the demise of an existing elite; the others referred to developments following the initial transfer of power, and were specified in terms of the classic progression from moderation through extremism and terror to peaceful consolidation first identified by Brinton.[11] The scope of Schwartz's study was thus wider than that of Geschwender in so far as it was not restricted to the explanation of the development of large-scale violence but went beyond this to analyze later stages of revolutions as well.

Schwartz interpreted the function of theorizing as the explanation of the conditions under which societies progressed from one stage of revolution to the next. The initial stage, he suggested, was one in which individuals became passively alienated from the political system. Individuals, he suggested, had cognitive structures involving images of themselves, of the polity and of appropriate political values, the last imparted in the process of political socialization. The link between these was that where individuals perceived the political system to be consonant with internalized political values, they would view the link between themselves and the political system in positive terms, i.e. regard it as legitimate; where, however, the polity was viewed as at odds with values, dissonance would ensue with consequent psychic tension. Individuals could alleviate this in two ways which would allow them to continue to perceive that the system was legitimate: they could modify their cognitions (by realigning political values to correspond to the system or dissociating an offending part of the system from the system itself) or adopt behaviours designed to alter the system in line with value-cognitions (become politically active and press for the reform of the system). Alternatively, individuals could downgrade the salience of politically-relevant cognitions, and hence reduce the level of dissonance associated with these cognitions. This involved a withdrawal of affection and legitimacy from the political system, from which individuals became passively alienated. Schwartz suggested that if, in the longer term, the political system was viewed as continually transgressing values, or proved to be incapable of reform, individuals who had originally coped with dissonance by cognitive modification or reform behaviour would eventually only be able to resolve dissonance by withdrawal and passive alienation.

Individuals could remain in this state, in which case the political system would continue to operate, but at a lower level of legitimacy; alternatively a 'change-agent' – a revolutionary organization or 'antisystem' – could emerge as an opposition to the political system in the second stage of revolution. Schwartz described two ways in which this could occur. Firstly, he suggested that, for the urban intelligentsia, passive alienation introduced a new source of cognitive dissonance because it conflicted with a normative cognition that the individual should participate in the polity, i.e. the intellectuals perceived a discrepancy between their 'real' withdrawal behaviour and the participatory behaviour they felt that they ought to adopt. Given this, they would attempt to reduce dissonance by participating in the polity. This supplied a motivation for individuals to create new political movements; these became revolutionary because intellectuals, uniquely, were able to articulate the causes of dissonance and discomfort in terms of deficiencies in social and political structures, and realize that dissonance-reduction would only be possible if these were changed. This directed them towards the formation of revolutionary organizations wherein they could participate (and diminish dissonance arising from non-participation) and which could be used to overthrow the existing regime and substitute one consonant with value-cognitions. The second mode of the creation of revolutionary organizations was where members of an existing organization active within the political system came to perceive eventually that the system could not be reformed to correspond with value-cognitions, and opted out to oppose the existing system itself and create a new one which would conform to values and hence reduce cognitive dissonance. Schwartz added a point concerning the leaders of such movements, that those who sought leadership positions would be those who were most highly motivated and energized, i.e. those suffering from the greatest cognitive dissonance.

The creation of revolutionary nuclei was a precondition for the third stage of revolution, the development of ideological appeals to the masses. Schwartz noted that there were four disparate audiences for such appeals: the passively alienated, those who had never been politically-conscious (the pre-politicals), those who remained participants in the existing system, and the personnel of the system itself. With regard to the first group, the movement had essentially to provide an explanation for dissonance in terms of the faults of the regime, induce a conviction that dissonance-reduction would follow upon the replacement of that regime, and permit the temporary alleviation of dissonance by encouraging tension-reducing behaviours, i.e. aggression manifested against the regime or a scapegoat. The pre-politicals were to be mobilized by adopting causes appropriate to them, by articulating long-felt grievances and demonstrating their political relevance. Supporters of the regime and its personnel were to be turned or neutralized by nurturing a cognition of the inevitability of revolutionary victory, thus inducing self-doubt as to regime-supporting behaviour and the perception that this was futile. If, at this stage, a revolutionary organization mobilized a critical minimum level of support it could proceed to the fourth stage of revolution, that of coalition and movement building. This involved the transformation of support for the movement into active and intense organized mass participation in its activities; psychologically, it included the total immersion of the masses in the movement to the extent that the individual abandoned his or herself or ego to become only a component of a monolithic organization. Schwartz characterized this as a response to passive withdrawal; this, as the individual became isolated from others, led to dissonance (as individuals had normative cognitions which stressed the desirability of a high level of interactions with others), which was reduced by the downgrading of the self (and hence the importance of contacts with others) and the substitution of an identity in terms of the totalitarian party. This contention was, of course, an attempt to recast the theory of mass society[12] – which purported to explain the growth and nature of mass adherence to totalitarian movements – within a cognitive framework.

The effect of a successful mobilization was to polarize society between the existing system and the revolutionary antisystem and usher in a stage of non-violent revolutionary politics as existing and contender elites competed for the support of the non-committed. Schwartz noted that it was possible, even at this eleventh hour, for political violence and indeed revolution to be avoided. If polarization was relatively weak, the system ultimately proved capable of adaptation, or the antisystem held to a non-violent ideology, then the antisystem party could be absorbed without revolution; if the elite was weak, it might abdicate power and leave the revolutionaries in control; if, however, none of these conditions were met, political violence would ensue as soon as leaders felt that they had a critical minimum of support for such behaviour from among their followers. Schwartz said surprisingly little about the latter, the sixth phase of revolution; but from the previous analysis it would appear that this involved leaders encouraging the masses to violence, violence which was cathartic in alleviating tensions arising from cognitive dissonance. The question as to the conditions under which such violence was or was not successful in overthrowing a regime was also ignored, and Schwartz passed on to a discussion of the course of revolutions.

Revolutionary movements had, in the pre-revolutionary phases, held out the promise of a Utopia following successful revolution, a Utopia in which social and political structures would be aligned to values, and in which individuals would feel psychological harmony. However, the moderates – the first elite to come to power following violence – were unable or unwilling to implement realignment quickly. This, Schwartz argued, implied that dissonance among the masses was not reduced, and led to a growth of support for extremists. The latter were distinguished from the moderates by greater initial levels of dissonance (the greater the tension, the more extreme the realignment of system and values necessary to alleviate it), as well as the desire to enjoy the rewards of power presently accruing to the moderates. The upshot of this was an extremist challenge to the new regime, the success of which was contingent upon the number of extremists and their degree of organization. The coming to power of the extremists was the eighth stage of revolution, and this was followed by the reign of terror. In this stage the extremists indulged in violence against the real or imagined, actual or potential enemies of the revolution, to alleviate dissonance; however, after a time, the terror fulfilled its cathartic function for most of the population, and attempts to continue it by a few leaders still suffering from extreme disturbance induced dissonance among the masses. This motivated attempts to end the terror and return to normality, the Thermidor reaction, and hence the revolution was completed.

FRUSTRATION-AGGRESSION THEORIES OF REVOLUTIONS

The mentors of the frustration-aggression variant of psychological theory were Dollard, Doob, Miller, Mowrer and Sears whose collaborative work[13] was first published in 1939. The essence of their argument was that aggression or aggressive behaviour was always a consequence of frustration. The latter was defined as 'that condition which exists when a goal-response suffers sudden interference', i.e. when people were prevented from achieving a desired objective. Such frustration automatically instigated aggression, defined as 'an act whose goal-response is injury to an organism',[14] the expression of which was cathartic, i.e. it relieved frustration. Dollard *et al.* posited a set of links between the degree of frustration and the level and target of consequent catharsis-inducing aggression. Low levels of frustration were productive of low levels of aggression and hence a limited need for catharsis; as there were costs attached to the direct expression of aggression against its perceived causes (because this was illegitimate and involved punishment), individuals would seek to express aggression by attacking other objects such as scapegoat groups or by sublimation into socially-modified behaviours. However, high levels of frustration led to high levels of aggression and a strong need to alleviate intense disturbance; in this context, the costs of attacking the source of frustration were minimal compared to the psychological advantages of catharsis, and aggression was directed against the primary cause of frustration. Dollard *et al.* noted that frustration-aggression theory had some implications for revolutionary behaviour. They suggested that Marx's contentions concerning the growth of proletarian revolutionary violence could be explained by the theory. Exploitation, alienation, the crises of capitalism and repression were productive of frustration initially expressed as blind aggression directed against the instruments of production, not the capitalists themselves. A continuing build-up of frustration to ever-higher levels caused by the inability of the system to respond positively eventually promoted a desperation in which the need for alleviation overcame social inhibitions and fears of state repression: the resulting mass expression of aggression toppled the capitalist class and the state it had commanded.

This hint as to the potential use of frustration-aggression theory in the context of revolutions was heeded by a number of theorists who sought to explain revolutions from a behaviouralist perspective, including James Davies.[15] His theory started from an apparent contradiction between various accounts of revolution provided by Marx and De Tocqueville. The former, Davies suggested, was most strongly associated with the thesis that revolutions followed from the immiseration of the industrial working class, with progressive degradation reaching the point of despair and inevitable revolt. However, Marx was also held to have explained revolutions in another way. Davies quoted a passage from an essay of Marx in which the latter seemed to suggest that revolutionary behaviour would also follow if there was a general improvement in economic conditions, but the workers perceived that their gains were not keeping pace with those made by capitalists, and revolted in consequence. This, it was argued, was generally compatible with De Tocqueville's theory of revolution as expressed in his book on France entitled *L'Ancien Régime*. He had suggested that oppression itself was not productive of revolutions: but, if oppression was lifted, even slightly, rebellion and revolution ensued. De Tocqueville explained this in terms of perceptions. Effective oppression encouraged people to believe that the existing state of affairs was inevitable, and discouraged attempts to challenge the existing order. An improvement shattered the myth of inevitable degradation and opened up the possibility of escape. Given this, conditions once accepted without question became intolerable and revolt followed.

The question for Davies was how to reconcile the contentions that, on the one hand, revolutions were caused by progressive immiseration, but on the other, that they stemmed from a progressive improvement in conditions of life. Davies suggested that this contradiction could be resolved by juxtaposing the observations of Marx and De Tocqueville into a new framework which would specify the causes of changes in the perceptions of individuals towards political regimes, and then using frustration-aggression theory to account for the link between such changes and the emergence of revolutionary behaviour. Thus Davies hypothesized that:

> Revolutions are most likely to occur when a prolonged period of objective economic and social development is followed by a short period of sharp reversal. The all-important effect on the minds of people in a particular society is to produce, during the former period, an expectation of continued ability to satisfy needs – which continue to rise – and then, during the latter, a mental state of anxiety and frustration when manifest reality breaks away from anticipated reality. The actual state of socio-economic development is such that past progress, now blocked, can and must continue for the future.[16]

Thus revolutions were preceded by a period of improvement, and this gave rise to expectations as to the continuing ability of the system to satisfy needs (De Tocqueville). However, there was a short, sharp reversal in which the system's ability to actually satisfy needs declined (Marx); the discrepancies between expectations and performance generated frustration which, if sustained, built up to very high levels and was eventually manifested in aggression against the regime (frustration-aggression theory). This gave rise to the so-called 'J' curve representation of the causes of revolutions (see Figure 2.1). The axes of the figure represent population needs and time;

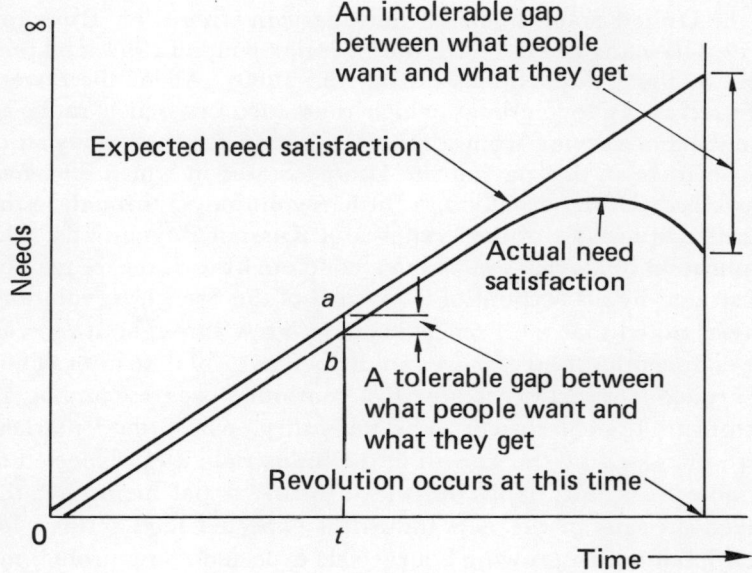

SOURCE: J. Davies, 'The "J" Curve of Rising and Declining Satisfactions as a Cause of Some Great Revolutions and a Contained Rebellion', in H. Graham and T. Gurr (eds), *Violence in America* (New York: Signet Books, 1969) p. 548.

FIGURE 2.1 *The 'J' curve theory of revolutions*

expectations are characterized by the straight line function, and increase linearly over time; the actual ability of the system to satisfy needs is shown by the quadratic function, which rises over much of its length and then dips sharply. Levels of discrepancy between expectations and performance such as those encountered at time t, i.e. of the magnitude ab, generate low frustration which, given the costs involved, is not expressed in aggression towards the regime, but sublimated or shifted on the scapegoats. However, the rapid growth of a very large gap between expectations and performance consequent upon sudden downturn of the latter generates very high levels of frustration, the alleviation of which outweighs any costs, and leads to aggression directed against the regime, to revolutionary behaviour.

Davies attempted to show that this model could be applied to a number of cases, including France in 1789, Dorr's rebellion in the United States in 1842, the American Civil War, Russia in 1917, Germany in the 1930s, the Egyptian coup of 1952, and race riots in the United States during the 1960s. All of these were referred to as revolutions, which thus encompassed a range of phenomena varying from a minor agitation for the extension of the suffrage in one part of the United States in which one man was killed (Dorr's rebellion, a 'little revolution'[17]) through to the massive upheavals of the French and Russian Revolutions. The application of Davies's model to a concrete historical case may be illustrated by his account of the causes of the French Revolution. Davies noted that the French economy grew throughout most of the eighteenth century, more rapidly before 1750 than after. This, he argued, created expectations of continued progress among all sectors in French society. The peasantry, whose food markets were increased by the growth of the industrial cities, expected to be able to acquire land and move up the social hierarchy; the skilled artisans in the new industries expected high returns for their labours; the growing bourgeoisie expected rising profits; the nobility looked for its share in the new wealth of France: all of these, and the regime itself, expected foreign conquests and the creation of an empire. These expectations were realized to a lesser and lesser degree in the 1760s and 1770s. The peasants found mobility blocked by feudal practices; the skilled artisans and the bourgeoisie were subject to high taxes on their wages and profits respectively; the nobility made some gains by regaining feudal rights, but felt that the regime fundamentally favoured the bourgeoisie: dreams of empire and conquest were dashed by defeat in 1763. However, any tendency for the gap between expectations and performance to widen was checked temporarily by the successful alliance with the American colonists in the War of Independence between 1778 and 1781, which provided a boost for the economy and morale, albeit at the price of raising future expectations to even higher levels. In the early and mid-1780s, the regime suffered from fiscal crisis, and was unable to sustain growth. The level of frustration engendered by this failure was not high enough to promote aggression against the regime; but when, in 1788–9, a combination of increased taxes, a bad harvest, delays in the payment of government debts and pensions, recession in textiles due to the trade treaty with England, rising bread prices, unemployment and a breakdown in the food supply system demonstrated a sudden and manifest reduction in the ability of the system to meet needs, the gap between expectations and performance widened dramatically. This produced high levels of intense frustration among almost all sections of French society, and this was transformed into aggression, into revolutionary violence which swept away the Ancient Regime. Davies provided similar accounts of the other revolutions, in each case fitting a 'J' curve to historical patterns prior to the revolution.

One problem with Davies's account was that it failed to provide a way of distinguishing between the causal processes involved in different types of revolutions, as to why revolutionary behaviour in one case took the form of a minor disturbance like Dorr's rebellion or in another was a full-blooded revolution like those in France and Russia. This, as well as the relatively few modern cases of revolution analyzed by Davies, was the starting point of a study by Tanter and Midlarsky.[18] They commenced their research by reviewing existing definitions of revolutions, following which they suggested a definition which would encompass the whole range of revolutionary phenomena, namely that a revolution was 'when a group of insurgents illegally and/or forcibly challenges the governmental elite for the occupancy of roles in the structure of political authority'.[19] Within this they delineated, again on the basis of the existing literature, four types of revolutions: mass revolutions, which involved significant popular participation in domestic violence sustained at a high level over a long period and which was undertaken in the interest of achieving fundamental changes in the structure of authority and in the social system; and palace revolutionary coups with lower levels of mass violence over a shorter period aimed at changing the polity but with limited social objectives; reform coups where there were low levels of violence lasting over a short to moderate period and directed only to the reform of the political system; and palace revolutions in which insurgent elites attempted to replace established elites in short actions involving minimal mass participation and violence. Tanter and Midlarsky noted that these revolutions constituted a hierarchy of revolutionary intensity, varying from the intense and prolonged violence which characterized mass revolutions to the limited and short-lived violence of the palace revolution. The object of their research was to explain variations in the scale of revolutionary intensity, why in some cases there were only palace revolutions, while in others reform coups or revolutionary coups or mass revolutions took place.

Two theories were outlined as potential explanations of this. One, deriving from Lipset,[20] related to educational levels among the population, and posited that there would be a negative relationship between the extent to which populations received formal education and the types of revolution, i.e. the higher the educational levels of a population, the lower the extent of revolutionary intensity. The other theory was adapted from Davies's basic model. While he had hypothesized that revolutions *per se* were a product of rising expectations coupled with a sudden and dramatic decline in a previously-improving performance, Tanter and Midlarsky suggested that the intensity and hence type of revolution would be a function of the magnitude of the gap between aspirations (extrapolations of current achievements into the future) and expectations (beliefs concerning the likely trend of future performance). Where this gap was small, the resulting levels of frustration would be limited, and consequent aggression would be minimal and last only a short time as catharsis would be quickly achieved; as the gap became wider, greater levels of frustration would be manifested in higher levels of aggression, and the more violent and sustained the insurrection would be. Thus palace revolutions would tend to occur when the gap was minimal, and the intensity of revolutions would increase with the magnitude of the gap until mass revolution occurred.

An attempt was made to investigate these theories using aggregate data on seventeen countries which had had successful revolutions between 1955 and 1960. The cases ranged from the De Gaulle coup in France in 1958 to the Cuban revolution. The dependent variable of revolutionary intensity was operationalized by two indicators: the number of deaths per million of the population in the revolution and the duration of violence. The former, based upon a count of reported deaths from revolutionary activities, was held to indicate the extent of violence and to be related to the objectives; a high number of deaths indicated that the revolution was aimed at greater political and social restructuring. The duration of the revolution was defined as the number of days between the outbreak of hostilities against an established regime to the time when the challengers took power. The independent variables were represented as follows: educational levels were measured as the proportion of the population aged between 5 and 14 years who were enrolled in primary schools; aspirations were conceived to be operationalized by the average rate of growth in GNP per capita over a seven-year period prior to the revolution; expectations were the extent of reversal of an upward growth trend just before the revolution. Thus a rising rate of growth in GNP was held to show rising aspirations, and a sudden change to negative growth to indicate falling expectations.

The testing of the aspirations/expectations hypothesis was considerably inhibited by the fact that in only one case – the Cuban revolution, the only mass revolution among their cases – exhibited the pattern of a rising rate of increase in GNP per capita followed by a sharp downturn just before the revolution occurred. In the others GNP increased consistently prior to the revolution, except in Argentina where GNP fell over this period. Tanter and Midlarsky provided a detailed analysis of the Cuban case, showing how GNP per capita had increased substantially over the period 1948–51, but declined dramatically in 1952–3, the latter year of which they took as the start of the Cuban revolution. Then, given the lack of a variable to represent expectations in cases apart from Cuba, they went on to examine the correlation between the other independent variables and the dependent ones. None of these proved to be statistically significant at any acceptable level which, the researchers considered, might have reflected the differential operation of the model between different regions of the world. They then disaggregated their cases by regions and recalculated their coefficients. This produced one correlation, that between rate of change in GNP and death rates, which was positive and significant among revolutions occurring in Asia and the Middle East; but the comparable correlation for Latin America was in a direction other than that hypothesized, and none of the correlations involving educational levels or the duration of the revolutions in any of the regions came within satisfactory error limits. Thus Tanter and Midlarsky were left with one substantive finding for two parts of the world, i.e. that there was a relationship between rising aspirations (as measured by rising rates of increase in GNP) and domestic violence (the death ratio) outside Latin America. They suggested that the latter exception reflected a pattern of revolutions peculiar to that continent, in particular the predominance of palace revolutions in which one section of the elite replace another without mass support or violence. The absence of violence, and hence of many deaths, meant that there was little variation for the independent variables to explain, and this was held to account for the poor statistical results obtained for revolutions in Latin America. In the other continents where palace revolutions were less prominent, the dependent variable of deaths per million had a wider range, and there was a strong correlation with rate of change in GNP.

The sum of Tanter and Midlarsky's results was then that (1) the aspirations/expectations theory was only verified for the case of mass revolution, (2) rising aspirations were correlated with death rates, except (3) in the case of palace revolutions particularly of the Latin American type. The researchers suggested that, in view of the final point, palace revolutions ought to be excluded from the general definition of revolutions as they were a qualitatively-different type of phenomenon which exhibited neither the levels of violence nor the dependence on aspirations of other types of revolutions. The researchers did not accept that the absence of a downturn in GNP just prior to the revolution (and hence of an expectations variable) among their cases apart from Cuba indicated the invalidity of Davies's theory as applied to reform and revolutionary coups. They argued that this reflected an error in variable specification, and that evidence of falling expectations would be found if other indicators were used. In particular, they extrapolated an argument from the work of Russett[21] that expectations as to land inequality might be important, although they failed to demonstrate the application of this within their original set of cases.

A third study which tried to incorporate the 'J' curve hypothesis was that of Bwy[22] upon revolutions in Latin America. He noted that revolutions on that continent referred to a multitude of disparate phenomena varying from the simple replacement of one leader by another (as in many coups) through to instances of major and prolonged violence (such as the Mexican revolution). Thus the set of events which had been termed revolutions was both 'eclectic' and 'unmanageable',[23] and Bwy suggested that it was necessary to differentiate between the various types and levels of behaviours involved. He attempted to do this by deriving data on various conflict events occurring in the provinces of a number of Latin American countries over a nine-year period which, following Rummel[24] and Tanter,[25] he then factor-analyzed to discover the existence of discrete clusters of events which were underlain by different dimensions of behaviours. Two such clusters were found. The first, which he labelled turmoil, involved anti-government riots, political clashes, demonstrations, strikes, injuries and assassinations, most of which suggested a kind of spontaneous, sporadic and non-organized dimension; the second, termed internal war, included guerilla warfare, terrorizing, sabotage and revolutionary invasion which, he argued, represented a dimension of aggression actions defined by high degrees of planning and organization.

Bwy then attempted to set out independent variables which could explain the incidence of these types of events, namely psychosocial dissatisfaction, legitimacy, and governmental responses to domestic conflict. The first of these was operationalized using survey data from samples of the populations of four Latin American countries: Brazil, Cuba, the Dominican Republic and Panama. The choice of these cases was dictated by the availability of data and there was clearly a question as to how representative these countries were of the continent as a whole. The data were derived by administering the Self-Anchoring Striving Scale, in which respondents were asked to describe their best and worst possible lives for the future, and then to define their current location, their location five years previously, and their expected location in five years' time, on scales where a score of 10 stood for their subjectively-defined optimum and 0 for the possible nadir of their fortunes. These scores, Bwy argued, could be used to define current levels of satisfaction and perceptions of changes compared to the past and expectations as to the future. The respondents were also asked to undertake the same exercise with respect to the past, present and future condition of their country. Bwy considered that these data could be used to indicate the perceived level of well-being when the survey was completed, and perceptions as to how this was changed from the past (which he termed personal or national satisfactions respectively) or was expected to change in the future (personal or national aspirations). The use of these variables would have enabled the testing of Davies's thesis (revolution following a perception that well-being had increased substantially over the period prior to the survey but that the future was bleak, this inducing a gap between aspirations and expectations from which frustration and aggression would develop), but Bwy found that neither of the variables measuring aspirations were suitable for inclusion in the model. His independent variables thus only related to satisfactions, to perceptions of well-being at the time of the survey and to the change in this compared to the recent past. Bwy then went on to define an independent variable of legitimacy, which was based in responses to the question on evaluations of the past, present and future condition of the nation, which had stressed political components: he also disaggregated governmental responses using a factor analysis and derived three dimensions of elite instability, the use of non-violent responses to strife and finally the use of coercion to repress disorder.

This variable and the dependent variable of type of conflict were organized so as to correspond to the survey in time, i.e. values were calculated for these variables over the four years prior to the survey and the four years following it, whereupon Bwy examined the set of possible regression coefficients using different combinations of independent variables and different time periods in order to derive a 'best' set of equations which could explain turmoil and internal wars. He concluded that, with respect to satisfactions, this variable was related to both types of conflict, but in different ways: low levels of present satisfactions, or a decline in satisfactions over the preceding period, were correlated with turmoil, while high present satisfactions and perceptions that well-being had increased were associated with internal wars. The legitimacy variable was found to be related to these types of conflict with, as expected, low levels of legitimacy being conducive to internal wars and the chances of this outcome diminishing with increasing levels of legitimacy. However, the influence of both of these perceptual variables was minimal compared to that of others in the model. The strongest relationships to be found were those between two of the components of governmental responses and conflict. While the coefficients for the use of violence to repress strife were too unstable to enable relationships to be specified, Bwy found that (1) current elite instability was strongly related to turmoil, while instability in the recent past was highly correlated with internal wars, and (2) non-violent governmental responses were associated with both turmoil and internal war, but much more strongly with the latter than the former.

A more comprehensive attempt to produce a theory of revolutions based in frustration-aggression theory, which incorporated some of the contentions of the 'J' curve model, was made by Gurr.[26] His central concern was to explain political violence, defined as 'all collective attacks within a political community against the political regime, its actors – including competing political groups as well as incumbents – or its policies'.[27] The set of such acts, he argued, could be scaled according to the scope of violence (the extent of popular participation in it), the intensity of violence (the destructiveness of violent action) and the duration of violence (the length of time for which it persisted). Using these, as well as the organizational dimension of types of violence identified theoretically by Eckstein[28] and empirically by Rummel, Tanter and Bwy, as noted earlier, Gurr derived a threefold typology of violence. This comprised, firstly, turmoil (relatively spontaneous, unorganized political violence with substantial popular participation, and including violent political strikes, riots, political clashes and localized rebellions); secondly, conspiracies (highly-organized violence with limited participation, examples of which were political assassinations, small-scale terrorism, small-scale guerilla wars, coups d'etat and mutinies); and thirdly internal wars (highly-organized, extensive political violence with widespread popular participation and the objective of overthrowing the regime or dissolving the state, and including large-scale terrorism, guerilla wars, civil wars and revolutions). Gurr did not discriminate between the categories of internal wars, i.e. for analytical purposes regarded them as referring to the same general phenomenon.

Gurr analyzed the determinants of these types of political violence in terms of (1) the factors variously influencing the potential for collective violence generally, (2) the chances that such violence would be politicized, and (3) the magnitude of any consequent political violence. With regard to the potential for collective violence, he specified the initial source of this as relative deprivation, defined as 'actors' perception of discrepancy between their value expectations and their value capabilities'.[29] Values were the desired events, objects and conditions for which men strived, and could be classified into welfare values (which referred to physical well-being and opportunities to use mental and physical abilities), power values (the extent to which men could influence others and avoid unwanted interference in their own actions) and interpersonal values (the psychological satisfactions achieved in non-authoritative social interactions). Value expectations were the average positions which actors considered they were justifiably entitled to; value capabilities were the average positions which actors perceived that they were likely to attain. Gurr, like Davies, argued that the development of a discrepancy between value expectations and capabilities, of relative deprivation, would lead to frustration, aggression and hence a potential for collective violence. However, unlike Davies, Gurr argued that there was no unique configuration of relative deprivation, i.e. that the 'J' curve was only one of a number of possibilities. Value expectations could change for a number of reasons, including the importation of new values from other societies (where, for example, as Deutsch[30] suggested, improvements in communications allowed the populations of poorer countries to compare their lot with that of those living in a richer one), the growth of new political ideologies, regime promises to end deprivation, or advances in the positions of salient reference groups. Value capabilities could stagnate or decline because of a poor resource base (for example where this was inadequate to provide for modernization, as advanced by the Feierabends[31]), elite unwillingness to share power, elite estrangement, or an inability for other reasons to match current performance with that achieved in the past. Given this, relative deprivation could take the forms of (a) decremental deprivation in which value expectations remained constant but capabilities declined; (b) aspirational deprivation where value capabilities were constant but expectations increased; and (c) progressive deprivation where expectations rose in line with capabilities over a period following which the latter declined. The third form was that specified by the 'J' curve: it may be noted that the first form, that of decremental deprivation, was independently identified by

Wertheim[32] as the pattern associated with the Indonesian revolution of 1945.

Thus relative deprivation which induced frustration and aggression led to a potential for collective violence, but obviously these could vary through different levels. Gurr suggested a number of factors which were associated with differences in the levels of intensity and scope of relative deprivation, and thence with the extent of frustration, aggression and violence. The intensity of relative deprivation was seen as a psychocultural variable, and determined by (1) the extent of the perceived discrepancy between value expectations and capabilities; (2) the salience of the values in question; (3) the number of alternative non-violent outlets for aggression; (4) the number of compensating satisfactions; (5) the time scale over which deprivation was experienced; and (6) the effectiveness of aggression in enhancing value capabilities in the short and medium terms. Deprivation would be the more intense the greater the gap between expectations and capabilities, the more salient were the values in question, the fewer the number of non-violent outlets, the fewer the number of satisfactions offsetting deprivations, the longer the time period over which deprivation was perceived to have been present, and the greater the effectiveness of the expression of aggression in stimulating improvements in performances. The scope of deprivation was a societal-level variable, and referred to the proportion of the population affected by deprivation. Where this was large, deprivation was more likely to lead to high levels of collective violence than where deprivation was confined to only a small section of the population.

The second set of factors identified by Gurr related to the determinants of the degree to which a potential for collective violence became a potential for political violence. This was held to be a function of two, basically cognitive, psychocultural variables, namely the intensities of normative and utilitarian justifications for political violence, as well as the variable of the scope of such justifications among the population. Normative justifications of political violence comprised the extent to which actors viewed violence as an appropriate means of conduct; utilitarian justifications related to how far actors saw violence as likely to achieve objectives, i.e. perceived that the adoption of violent behaviour would pay off in terms of an improvement in value capabilities. Gurr suggested that the intensity of normative justifications was a function of six factors: (1) the extent to which collective violence of any kind was normal in a society (the more populations resorted to this, the higher the chance that an extension to the political arena would be regarded as acceptable); (2) the degree to which there was a specific tradition of political violence (the absence of this psychologically inhibited the deployment of such violence, the presence of a tradition meant that there were few or no internal sanctions); (3) the nature of dominant modes of socialization (whether these involved coping with aggression by intrapunative or extrapunative means, the former associated with the turning of aggression towards the self, the latter to expressing it on external targets, including the regime); (4) regime legitimacy (where individuals were strongly psychologically-bonded to the regime, violence was less likely than where such ties were weak or non-existent); (5) revolutionary appeals (how far political movements were able to convince actors that the source of their frustrations lay in the political system and were successful in constructing a normative justification for violence against that system); and (6) the intensity of utilitarian justifications for violence (the more effective violence was, the more likely that normative justification of it was to be found). The latter relationship was two-way: Gurr also suggested that the strength of normative justifications was a determinant of that of utilitarian ones (the greater the normative justification for violence, the greater the chance that it would be perceived as effective). The other determinants of utilitarian justifications were: previous regime effectiveness in dealing with deprivation (if the regime previously proved able to adapt, aggression would be suspended in the shorter term to allow the modification of policy or personnel; if the regime had been intransigent, actors would be inclined to look for immediate pay-offs from violence); the success of other groups or the actor's own group when political violence had previously been deployed (which related to the extent that violence would be effective in alleviating aggression and achieving an increase in regime capabilities); the density of aggressive symbols in the media (the extent to which the media impressed the use of violence as an effective means of catharsis and of promoting change); the nature of regime responses to deprivation (the differential allocation of resources between relatively-deprived groups would intensify frustration among losers and encourage them to believe that change was necessary in order to secure a just share of resources); finally the intensity of utilitarian justification was related to the utilitarian content of the appeals of political movements, to the quantitative level of positive or negative pay-offs for violence offered as compared to those available from the regime. These various factors collectively determined whether, and to what intensity, violence was cognized to be justified by individuals, and explained the extent to which they were psychologically able and willing to express violence against the regime or were inhibited from so doing. The other variable of the scope of justifications referred to the extent to which support for violence on normative or utilitarian grounds was widespread or confined among the population. Gurr suggested that the higher the historical levels of political violence, the lower the degree of regime legitimacy, and greater the past success of groups in obtaining pay-offs from political violence, the more ineffective the regime's past ability to alleviate deprivation, and the greater the proportion of available media sources promoting aggressive symbols, the larger the part of the population which believe that political violence was justified, and the higher the level of potential for political violence.

The magnitude of actual political violence was held to be a function of two other clusters of variables, institutional support and coercive control, and the distribution of these between regimes and challengers. The degree of institutional support available to either of these was a product of the extent to which the population was included within institutions, how far these were complex and cohesive, the resources available to them, and the number and variety of opportunities and channels for participation. A high level of institutional support was where one side or another had institutions which involved a large section of the population, were both complex and cohesive, commanded access to substantial resources, and included established and multiple modes of participation; a low degree of institutional support was present if the scope of institutions was limited and these were simple, non-cohesive, with few resources and restricted chances for participation or channels for popular involvement. Gurr regarded changes in institutional support as having a zero-sum product, i.e. any gain by one side was matched by a loss for the other. Coercive control was conceived of in the same way. This comprised, for both the regime and dissidents, the extent to which they had the population under surveillance, the sizes and resources of their militaries, and the loyalty of their respective armed forces. Additionally, for the regime, coercive control depended upon the severity and consistency of coercion. Gurr suggested that the relationship between the severity of regime violence and non-regime political violence was curvilinear, that low levels of regime violence would be associated with low mass political violence, but that rising levels of the former would cause rising levels of the latter up to a point beyond which repression would become so severe that counter-violence would diminish and perhaps vanish. Thus regime coercive control depended in some measure upon the willingness and the ability of the regime to consistently escalate coercion to levels high enough to repress opposition almost completely. It may be noted that Gurr regarded repression to such levels as having a 'feedback effect': such repression might suppress violence, but it would also intensify discontent, create new discontent, reduce regime legitimacy, and provide highly visible targets for violence. Thus, in the longer run, high levels of repression would be counterproductive. On the dissident side, levels of coercive control were also held to depend upon the extent to which political movements were able to achieve a concentration in geographical areas isolated enough to give immunity from destruction by the armed forces of the regime. Thus a high degree of regime control involved the regime having authority over the bulk of the population and a large, loyal and effective military which could be deployed if necessary to maximal levels of repression; a low degree of such control over coercion implied a limited authority, and a small, disloyal or ineffective military which could not sustain increasing repression. A high degree of dissident control involved the same conditions as for high regime control, plus ability to hold a base area, a lack of which coupled with limited undisciplined forces with few resources characterized a low degree of control.

The relationship between these variables and the magnitude of political violence was held to vary generally according to the balance of institutional support/coercive control between the regime and the dissidents. Where the regime had a substantial balance of support and control, the level of political violence would be low; the latter would be higher if dissidents were able to gain a greater share of support and control; the maximum level of political violence would occur where the balance was appropriately equal, and it was vital for both sides to win in order to determine the outcome of the insurrection. Thus, within the range of the balance of support/coercion being either in the regime's favour or approaching equality between the sides, Gurr generally posited a linear relationship between the ratio of regime support/coercion and dissident support/coercion and the level of political violence. This general specification was subject to one caveat, which related to the severity of repression component of coercive control. It was noted earlier that the relationship between this and the level of violence was hypothesized to be curvilinear in the shorter term, i.e. that increased repression begat increased violence up to a point following which further repression resulted in diminishing political violence. Clearly this variable could operate over part of the range of ratios between regime and dissident support/coercion, and result in lower levels of political violence than would be predicted by the other components of these variables. A group of dissidents could, for example, have won levels of institutional support and gained some control of the means of coercion, which would predict a particular magnitude of political violence; but, if the regime was prepared and able to use the remainder of its armed forces to repress thoroughly, the actual level of violence might be considerably lower. Thus the general linear projection of variable relationships was subject to the operation of the non-linear relationship between severity of repression and political violence although, as has been seen, severe repression would, in the longer run, engender a higher potential for political violence.

Gurr noted that these relationships would be similar in the (relatively rare) cases where dissidents held the balance of institutional support/coercive control. Where the balance was minimally in favour of the dissidents, there would be high levels of political violence as regimes strived to sustain themselves; the more the balance was in favour of the dissidents, the lower the levels of political violence. As in the previous case, severity of repression, this time by the dissidents, had a potential 'bending' effect on the relationship between other variables and the magnitude of violence, with dissidents, once they were able to exert a high degree of coercive control, being able to minimize violent opposition by maximum repression. Unfortunately, this point, which has an obvious relevance to explaining the course of successful revolutions, was not developed by Gurr, although it could, for example, provide an explanation for some of the stages of the course of revolutions identified by Brinton.[33]

This analysis was then related to Gurr's initial typology of the forms of political violence, namely those of turmoil, conspiracy and internal war. The likelihood of turmoil was maximal where (1) there was relative deprivation and consequent frustration limited in scope to masses but absent among elites (the latter defined as individuals with the acquired or inherited personal characteristics which were culturally-prescribed requisites for high-value positions, regardless of whether these had been attained); (2) the perception of deprivation extended to only a few values; (3) the regime held the dominant balance of institutional support/coercive control, and dissidents were concentrated in areas under the regime's control; the corollary of this was (4) that dissidents had low institutional support and a low degree of coercive control, in particular they lacked possession of a 'base' area within which they were immune from attack. Under these conditions, there was a high probability that aggression arising from frustration would take the form of episodic, unstructured and unorganized violence, of turmoil. Conspiracy was most likely where: (1) relative deprivation was low or mild among the masses, but high among elites; (2) deprivation among elites extended over a wide range of values, and particularly included discontent with respect to power values; (3) the regime held the balance of institutional support and coercive control but (4) the dissidents as an elite were able to develop tight-knit organizations which offered some basis for sustained activities. Given this configuration, dissident elites would, Gurr argued, be limited in the short term to trying to achieve power by subverting the military, as there was little basis for mass mobilization. If this strategy proved unfruitful because of military adherence to the regime, conspiratorial groups might adopt a longer-term strategy of terrorism or small-scale guerilla warfare designed to increase mass discontent and provide an ultimate basis for the mobilization of the masses in an internal war. This was most probable when (1) relative deprivation was intense among both masses and elites; (2) it extended over a wide range of values; (3) where dissidents had, following a period of turmoil and conspiracy, garnered levels of institutional support and coercive control approaching those of the regime; and (4) were concentrated in areas outside the control of the regime's armed forces which facilitated both the extension of institutional support and the expansion of coercive control. The third condition implied that there were means by which dissidents could transform turmoil or conspiracy into internal war, and Gurr tentatively sketched the outlines of the processes involved. Dissidents could attempt to raise mass levels of relative deprivation by intensifying existing expectations or creating new ones or they could try to further politicize deprivations by widening and deepening the media's presentation of aggressive symbols; regimes could defend themselves by adapting their policies to lessen deprivations, tightening control over the media, extending the scope of regime institutions, or increasing coercion. These regime responses could, however, backfire. Concessions to dissidents could raise the intensity of utilitarian justifications of violence, greater control over the media would not be acceptable in a society accustomed to a relatively free media, including new sections of the population within institutions might upset established patterns of interactions and create discontent, and repression, as noted earlier, would prove a stimulus to greater violence in the longer term. Thus regime responses could result in a stronger impetus towards political violence among populations, and shifts of institutional support and coercive control towards the dissidents which, in turn and subject to the uses made of resources by the latter, generated further political violence.

Gurr not only created this elaborate, complex and comprehensive theory of political violence, but also made an empirical investigation[34] of some of the hypotheses stemming from it. This was based upon data collected on 114 polities which had populations of one million or more in 1962. The data, which was aggregate in character, included a large number of social, economic and political indicators as well as measures of civil strife over the period 1961–5 inclusive. The dependent variable of the magnitude of civil strife comprised data derived from newspapers and digests on the pervasiveness of strife (an estimate of the number of participants in strife events per 100 000 of the population), the duration of strife (number of days over which strife had occurred), and the intensity of strife (dead and injured in strife events per 10 000 000 of the population). These were combined to give strife scores, which were calculated separately for instances of turmoil, conspiracy and internal war events and aggregated to give a total strife score. With regard to the independent variables, Gurr initially specified a simplified version of the causal processes outlined in the complex theory just discussed, namely that there was a basic relationship between relative deprivation and civil strife, which was mediated by five other sets of variables relating to coercive potential, institutionalization, facilitation and legitimacy. Deprivation was divided into two types. Firstly, there was persisting deprivation, which operated over a long time scale, and was operationalized in terms of aggregate indicators of the scope and intensity of economic discrimination, political discrimination, potential separatism, dependence on foreign capital, extent of religious cleavages and lack of educational opportunity. The second category of deprivation – short-term deprivation – was represented by seven indicators, relating to trends in trade values (one the change in this 1957–60 compared to 1950–7, the other the change between 1960 and 1965 compared to 1950–62), inflation 1960–3 compared to 1958–61, GNP in the early 1960s compared to the 1950s, other adverse economic conditions (bad harvests, drought, slumps in export markets) and new value-depriving policies of governments 1960-3, policies which removed privileges from particular groups within societies, such as land reforms, tax increases or limitations on civil liberties.

The intervening variable of coercive potential and size of coercive forces comprised four factors: the military participation ratio (military personnel per 10 000 of the population), the internal security participation ratio (internal security personnel per 10 000 of the population), a scale score for the frequency of military interventions against the regime in the recent or distant past, and an indicator of the extent of military or police participation in strife over the 1961–5 period.

Two variables were derived from these, one comprising a combination of the two participation ratios (size of coercive forces), the other a composite of all four variables which gave a total coercive potential score. The institutionalization factor was measured as the ratio of labour union membership to non-agricultural employment (presumably as an indicator of extent of institutionalization among the workforce), government expenditure as a proportion of Gross Domestic Product (on the hypothesis that the more the government spent, the greater its intervention in economic and social life, and therefore the larger the number of institutions in society), and scales representing the stability of the party system. The third mediating variable, facilitation, was indexed as past civil strife, those levels which had occurred 1946–59, and social and structural facilitation, the latter including scores for the extent to which territories were suitable for guerilla warfare, the numerical strength and status of communist parties, and the extent to which strife attracted foreign support and to what level this was made available. The final variable was legitimacy, for which Gurr coded scales of the origins, characters and durability of national institutions and combined these into an overall measure.

These independent variables were, with one exception, hypothesized to be related to strife by a function with a linear form. The exception was the size of coercive forces which, following his earlier theoretical exposition, Gurr postulated should have a curvilinear relationship with strife over the shorter term but, because of the feedback effects of large-scale repression, induce further strife in the long term. He found that this appeared to be the case. Among the whole set of polities, there was a tendency for strife to rise initially with size of coercive forces, then decline as the latter rose, then increase once more as size of forces approached very high levels. When, however, he eliminated cases from his data which had a long history of strife (and countries facing foreign threats which had large militaries for reasons unrelated to internal conflict) he found that the relationship between strife and coercive force was, as predicted by the short-term analysis, best fitted by a quadratic equation, i.e. strife increased with size of military and then, as the latter rose, the former declined. The fact that the relationship conformed to the short-term prediction among these, but strife increased at the highest levels of coercive force size when countries with long histories of political violence were included in the data set, was taken as a prima-facie validation of the contention that high levels of repression initially dampened down violence, but in the longer term begat further violence. Gurr then went on to examine both the sample and the partial correlations between the independent variables and the total magnitude of strife, and the magnitudes of turmoil, conspiracy and internal wars. With respect to the total magnitude of civil strife, it was found that the values of the simple correlation coefficients were in the hypothesized directions, but some of the relationships were considerably modified by controlling for the mediating effects of other independent variables. In particular, the inclusion of the facilitation variable reduced the partial correlation between past strife and current strife to a value near 0; coercive potential mediated the relationship between legitimacy and strife, while leaving legitimacy with some independent influences; the inclusion of the effects of both coercive potential and facilitation acted to nullify the correlation between institutionalization and strife, and to severely reduce that between short-term deprivation and strife. After controlling for these interrelationships, Gurr found that the most important factor was facilitation, this being followed in order of variance in strife explained by persisting deprivation, short-term deprivation, legitimacy and coercive potential. The magnitude of the weighting of these may be pointed out in that facilitation on its own explained as much of the variance as all of the other independent variables put together, its explanatory power being twice that of the next variable, persisting deprivation, four times that of short-term deprivation or legitimacy, and twelve times that of coercive potential.

A similar analysis of appropriate partial correlation coefficients was undertaken for each of the forms of strife, the findings of which lent some credence to Gurr's theory of the causes of turmoil, conspiracy and internal wars. Persisting deprivation was associated with all of these but, within this, political deprivation was more strongly related to conspiracy than to the other forms of violence. There were correlations between short-term deprivation and all of the categories of political violence, but the coefficient was considerably higher for internal wars than for the other categories. With respect to the intervening variables: (1) institutionalization had virtually no impact upon any of the forms of political violence when its interrelationships with other independent variables were controlled for; (2) legitimacy was most highly correlated with turmoil, weakly related to conspiracy and unrelated to internal wars; (3) coercive potential was weakly related to all of the types of strife, more strongly to internal war than the others; and (4) among the components of facilitation, past strife levels were correlated weakly with turmoil although not internal war or conspiracy, but social and structural facilitation was very highly related to internal war, weakly related to conspiracy, and appeared insignificant in explaining turmoil. Overall the factors most closely associated with turmoil were persisting deprivation, a past history of civil strife, low legitimacy, and an absence of social and structural facilitation. Conspiracy was most strongly associated with persisting deprivation, particularly political deprivation, and some degree of social and structural facilitation; internal war was associated with a combination of persisting deprivation and short-term deprivation, coercive potential, and considerable social and structural facilitation. There was a prima-facie fit between these findings and Gurr's hypotheses set out on pp. 78–9, although Gurr himself did not pursue this in his article. While he was unable to specify empirically the extent to which relative deprivation was mass- or elite-based, it was apparent that, as suggested, political deprivation was more important in conspiracy than in turmoil or internal war, and there was a relationship between the magnitude of the indicators of deprivation and types of strife, with persisting deprivation on its own producing turmoil or conspiracy, but when this was accompanied by short-term deprivation which raised the overall level of relative deprivation to higher levels, internal war resulted. Among the variables mediating between deprivation and strife, the association between social and structural facilitation and types of strife was as predicted, low facilitation being related to turmoil, moderate facilitation to conspiracy and high facilitation to internal war. Coercive potential similarly fitted theoretical expectations, as it was lowly correlated with turmoil and conspiracy reflecting the fact that the latter took place predominantly in societies with a high coercive potential (i.e. there was little variation in the independent variable) but more highly correlated with internal war (reflecting variations in the extent to which regimes had lost control of coercive resources). The finding for legitimacy fitted well with Gurr's progression from turmoil and conspiracy to internal war, the relationship between this variable and strife being relatively stronger at the lower levels of the latter, and of limited relevance to internal war by which time regimes had become delegitimized to a marked extent (there thus being little variation in legitimacy to be associated with internal war). The only major finding not supporting the theory was the poor explanatory value of institutionalization, reflecting the fact that the effects of this were mediated through other variables.

Gurr concluded his study by making three general claims for his empirical research. Firstly, this had provided the first clear evidence of the relationship between coercive force and strife which, as has been noted, demonstrated that increasing size would in the short run be associated with rising then falling violence, but in the long run was a cause of further violence. Secondly, the consistency with which the indicators of relative deprivation had been associated with strife was held to provide validation of the importance of this variable, which was of course linked to violence by the frustration-aggression psychological theory. Finally, the fact that the deprivation indicators as well as the other proxy variable for perceptions, legitimacy, had explained a considerable proportion of the variance in strife showed that perceptual variables which gave rise to frustration and aggression had to be accorded a central place in accounting for political violence.

AN EVALUATION OF PSYCHOLOGICAL THEORIES OF POLITICAL VIOLENCE AND REVOLUTIONS

The central problem with all of the theoretical and empirical work which has been outlined in this chapter was the absence of any direct evidence concerning the relationship between perceptions, psychological processes and political violence among individuals. None of the six theorists was able to present data derived from studies of individuals which demonstrated the basic causal mechanisms specified in the various models: all of them inferred that psychological variables intervened between perceptions and violence. Geschwender and Schwartz simply showed that it was theoretically plausible to explain political violence and revolutions in terms of the cognitive dissonance theory; Davies inferred that the relationship between historical development and revolutions reflected the operation of mass frustration-aggression; Tanter and Midlarsky suggested that the coincidence of political violence in Cuba in 1953 and a rising, then steeply declining, rate of change in GNP was explicable in terms of a gap between expectations and aspirations which had generated frustration and aggression. Bwy assumed that any relationship between changes in satisfactions and turmoil or internal war was caused by psychological processes; Gurr inferred that correlations between aggregate-level variables representing relative deprivation and aggregate indicators of levels of political violence were a product of frustration and aggression among individuals.

This absence of direct data implied, firstly, that there was no way of verifying which of the psychological variants utilized was appropriate, or the conditions under which one or the other, or indeed both, would tend to hold. Thus it is not known whether the psychological mechanisms linking perceptions and behaviour were primarily cognitive or through frustration and aggression. Secondly, within each of the psychological theories, it was not possible to be certain of the nature of the psychological processes involved. There was a divergence between the two cognitive dissonance theorists as to the initial response to dissonance by individuals. Geschwender saw dissonance as engendering psychic tension and claimed that this directly motivated behaviour designed to bring the real world and reality-based cognitions into line with normative ones; Schwartz described tension as producing withdrawal or passive alienation, the translation of which into political violence was contingent upon the extent to which revolutionary movements with a violent ideology succeeded in explaining, articulating and mobilizing dissonance. A similar division was apparent among the frustration-aggression theorists. Davies, Tanter and Midlarsky and Bwy all specified a direct relationship between frustration and political violence; Gurr saw the relationship between these as mediated by a cluster of variables which influenced the scope and intensity of normative and utilitarian justifications of political violence. Thus to Geschwender, Davies, Tanter and Midlarsky and Bwy the necessary psychological condition for political violence was dissonance or frustration; Schwartz and Gurr specified other psychological conditions which had to be fulfilled before political violence would occur. The lack of individual-level psychological data meant that it was not possible to decide between these different accounts of the kinds of psychological processes involved in political violence.

The third, and perhaps most serious, consequence of this problem was that there was no way of discerning whether the links between perceptions and political violence comprised psychological mechanisms at all. If, of course, there was general agreement that violence was *always* a manifestation of aggression induced by frustration or that it *always* constituted dissonance-reducing behaviour this would not matter. However, it has been shown experimentally by Milgram[35] that violence could occur *without* prior frustration or cognitive dissonance and, further, there are a number of other theories of violence which suggest that this may be caused by non-psychological factors. Violence may be undertaken at the behest of an authority figure;[36] it may be imitative; it may reflect simple indignation, as Lupsha[37] has suggested; political violence may be the only means of achieving goals as, for example, where established elites make a 'non-decision'[38] to exclude the demands of particular groups from the political agenda; political violence may be deployed as the most effective means of achieving goals (i.e. Gurr's set of variables relating to utilitarian justifications of political violence may constitute independent variables in their own right, and not simply mediate between a general potential for violence engendered by frustration and the expression of aggression in the political sphere); violence may be a normal form of political behaviour in many societies (in which case Gurr's factor of normative justifications for violence would constitute an independent variable influencing political violence); political violence among the masses may be straightforward self-defence against attacks by the forces of the regime. It is possible, at least in principle, to utilize one or more of these various alternative explanations to provide other theories of political violence, and to account for associations or correlations between historical developments or aggregate-level variables. Against this, the only defence of the psychological theorists was that of an assertion of the primacy of psychological variables.

It may also be pointed out that, even if the empirical studies of the psychological theorists were to be interpreted in terms of the operation of 'state of mind' variables, the more sophisticated analyses suggested that the influence of these upon political violence was limited relative to that of other non-psychological variables. Thus Bwy's survey/aggregate data study found a correlation between changes in satisfactions and the incidence of violence, but this was trivial in magnitude compared to the comparable correlations between the various components of governmental responses and political violence. Gurr's complex causal model of civil strife also indicated that perceptual/psychological variables were a factor in explaining violence, but the social and structural facilitation variables accounted for a considerably greater proportion of the total variance, particularly in the case of internal wars. The findings of these two theorists were, however, at odds with those of Davies and Tanter and Midlarsky, whose empirical analyses were held to indicate that perceptual/psychological factors were dominant in explaining revolutions. But the procedures adopted in these studies were, to say the least, open to question. Davies attempted to validate the 'J' curve by demonstrating that, over a range of cases, there was a 'fit' between historical developments prior to revolutions, and the pattern of expectations/performances predicted by his theory. It is apparent from the case studies that the 'J' curve could operate over a very elastic time scale: its effects were identified for France over a period of eighty years, for Dorr's rebellion and the Russian Revolution over sixty years, and for the Egyptian revolution over thirty years. Tanter and Midlarsky widened the range even further by adducing a 'J' curve process for Cuba over a period of four years. This very considerable degree of variation left these theorists open to the charge that, with any particular revolution, it would be possible to derive a 'J' curve simply by varying the time period; evidence of growth and then decline could be found for most societies over a period of up to a century before a revolution. Further, even if this difficulty was overcome, it would still be necessary to make strong assumptions in order to argue that whatever revolutionary violence had occurred at a particular point was wholly, or even largely, a product of the perceptual/psychological processes specified by the 'J' curve and indicated by a particular configuration of historical circumstances. It is at least theoretically possible that political violence could have occurred for reasons unrelated to these, and the *ex post facto* derivation of a 'J' curve effect would then constitute a misinterpretation of the causes of such violence. The importance of the time scale of the 'J' curve and the problems of inference were well illustrated by Tanter and Midlarsky's explanation of the Cuban revolution. They presented data on changes in GNP per capita and noted that this had increased rapidly over the period 1948 to 1952, and then declined steeply in 1953, the year they took as the starting point of the revolution. The rising rate of increase in GNP per capita was held to define rising aspirations, the sudden decline falling expectations, and the development of a gap between these created frustration which was transmuted into aggression expressed as violence against the Batista regime. However, there was no explosion of mass violence in 1953, only Castro's first armed landing, and the small-scale and abortive attack on the

Moncada barracks which was notable precisely because it did not stimulate mass attacks on the existing regime. In fact, such mass violence as did occur in Cuba started in 1957, when the efforts of Castro and his guerilla band in the Sierra Maestra began to be supplemented by urban violence in Havana. This would not affect Tanter and Midlarsky's account if the Cuban economy had continued to decline after 1953, in which case they could argue that the gap between aspirations and performance was widening and frustration increasing up to a point at which action became imperative: but, in fact, the Cuban economy recovered substantially in the mid-1950s to the extent that by 1957 economic growth and GNP per capita had risen to record levels.[39] On the 'J' curve hypothesis, this ought to have reduced the chances of political violence as the gap between aspirations and expectations was reduced, but it was precisely at this juncture that the major political violence started to occur. The implication of this was that Tanter and Midlarsky's analysis depended critically upon the time period chosen, and upon the assumption that any violence occurring after the end of it must have reflected the processes identified by the 'J' curve: if the time scale was lengthened it was apparent that the relationship between the economic variable and violence was in fact contrary to that hypothesized in the 'J' curve, and that the violence must therefore have been caused by other factors. Thomas's[40] historical account suggested that these included both self-defence against the increasing repression of the Batista regime and tactical violence designed to intimidate and disable the regime. Considerations such as these suggest that the empirical demonstrations of the 'J' curve by Davies and Tanter and Midlarsky must be treated with some caution, as must their assertions that perceptual/psychological variables were critical in explaining revolutions. Additionally, with respect to the 'J' curve itself, it may be noted that the only empirical evidence for its operation was that provided by the studies which have just been criticized: neither Bwy nor Gurr found 'J' curve patterns as such in their analyses, although the former found rising satisfactions appeared to be associated with internal wars (but was unable to identify a downturn effect), while the latter found that short-term deprivation was correlated with internal wars (but was unable to specify whether this was preceded by a rising, constant or falling trend in performances).

The final point concerns the relationship between the focus of the psychological theories, the explanation of the emergence, magnitude or course of political violence, and their value in explaining revolutions. The theories offer accounts of the causes and nature of political violence; but these would only constitute explanations of revolutions if either revolutions were equated with political violence generally, or regarded as a form of political violence. Davies and Tanter and Midlarsky took the former tack and effectively defined revolutions as co-extensive with political violence. Bwy noted that, in the Latin American context, revolution had been used to describe all kinds of political violence, and accepted that explanations of the latter were also explanations of the former. Gurr, by way of contrast, regarded revolutions as one instance of a general form of political violence, that of internal war. Revolutions were subsumed into this category along with civil wars, guerilla wars and large-scale terrorism, and it was effectively assumed that explanations of the scale, scope and magnitude of political violence at the internal-war level were also explanations of the variants of internal wars. The two other psychological theorists dissented from these approaches. Geschwender was careful to distinguish between the component of revolutions involving mass political violence, which he argued could be explained in terms of a theory relating to the emergence of social movements in general, and the component of processes which developed after initial mass violence, which was not amenable to explanation in such terms. The latter processes were not specified but it was clear that Geschwender considered that there was more to revolutions than political violence. Schwartz made a similar distinction, with revolutions divided into pre-violent stages (the first five in his schema), the stage of the outbreak of revolutionary violence, and what he described as the post-violent stages (stages seven to ten). The apparent implication of the last set of stages was that revolutions did not merely involve political violence, but the successful overthrow of regimes and the completion of processes prior to the consolidation of a new regime. It may, however, be noted that one of the stages included under the post-violent heading was the reign of terror, which Schwartz in fact treated as a second phase of political violence. While this must qualify the degree to which he was seen to be disposed to argue that revolutions required explanation of a wider range of phenomena than political violence, it did not, in the author's opinion, entirely vitiate Schwartz's rejection of a pure focus upon violence as accounting for revolutions. Even given this, large-scale political violence was not the only defining condition for revolutions: revolutions additionally involved regime changes and other post-violent and non-violent stages.

Clearly, the acceptance of one notion or another about what it was necessary to explain to account for revolutions implied different evaluations of the psychological theories. If this was conceived of purely in terms of political violence, or as a component of political violence, all of the theories would constitute full theories of revolutions; if, however, revolutions were defined as having other characteristics or as involving other processes, the psychological theorists, with the exception of Schwartz, could only be regarded as having produced partial theories of revolutions. There are of course no objective criteria for suggesting that one of these conceptions of revolutions was correct and the other wrong, but it is worth noting that the association between political violence and revolutions which was apparent in the work of most of the psychological theorists (and which was one of the main factors distinguishing their contribution from that of other theorists whose approach lay within the other disciplines of the social sciences) was held to have both advantages and disadvantages. Two advantages could be cited. Firstly, it was claimed that treating revolutions within the framework of political violence meant that they could be incorporated within the behaviouralism paradigm for research in political science. The importance of this lay in the contention supported by many political scientists in the 1960s that behaviouralism would prove to be the key to the development of the study of politics in a unified and properly scientific manner; in order to achieve this, it was necessary to redefine political phenomena such as revolutions within the corpus of the behaviouralist approach. Secondly, it was argued, notably by Eckstein,[41] that the focus upon a single behavioural dimension emphasized the common elements of the range of phenomena which included riots, rebellions, terrorists, civil wars and revolutions and avoided the study of these in isolation. Thus it was claimed that the 'second wave' theorists, who concentrated solely upon the so-called 'Great Revolutions', had neglected the study of other forms of political violence with the consequences that (1) such forms of violence remained unexplained; (2) theorists were unable to specify why political violence took the form of riots or rebellions rather than revolutions; and (3) there was no understanding of the links between levels of violence. With regard to the last point, it was noted that revolutions were often preceded by lesser forms of violence, and clearly the latter were a contributory factor to the former, and their causes and effects required explanation if revolutions were to be accounted for adequately.

The disadvantages of the approach adopted by most of the psychological theorists were the converse of the points made above. In the late 1960s and the 1970s, behaviouralism came under attack[42] on the grounds that it embodied an inherently conservative approach to the study of politics and that its claims to science were unjustified. In the context of revolutions, it could be argued that the stress upon individual-level psychological processes took no account of the macro-structural context: revolutions were portrayed as a manifestation of uncontrollable frustration and aggression or cognitive dissonance rather than as arising from structured inequalities in wealth, power and status between different groups in societies. The former view was held to obscure the essential radical nature of revolutions which was, of course, embodied in the structurally orientated theories. With respect to methodology, it was debatable as to whether the empirical studies of the psychological theorists were any more 'scientific' than those of other theorists, given their dependence upon aggregate data to represent the perceptions of individuals (except in Bwy's study) or their behaviours and the purely inferential status of the contention that the relationship between these aggregate variables represented psychological processes. With regard to the second alleged advantage of approaching revolutions through the medium of political violence, the counter-argument could be made that this rendered revolution virtually meaningless as a concept. If revolutions were just political violence, the word was redundant; likewise if it was simply equated with civil war or large-scale terrorism as internal wars there was no need for a separate concept of `revolution. For revolution to be a useful term, it had to retain unique characteristics, in particular its original association with the successful overthrow of regimes and subsequent attempts to implement social changes. The point may be made by reference to Russia in 1905 and 1917 and thereafter. Under the definitions of Davies, Tanter and Midlarsky, Bwy and Gurr, the violence in both of these periods would qualify them as revolutions or internal wars: but clearly there was a substantive difference between the events of 1905 and 1917, both in terms of their failure and success and because the 1917 insurrection was followed by major structural changes, and it could be argued that this should be recognized by referring to 1905 as a revolt or rebellion and 1917 as a revolution. To ignore these differences was to treat qualitatively discrete phenomena as if they were the same.

Thus it can be suggested that the psychological theories were deficient in that they did not include individual-level data demonstrating the existence of psychological processes linking perceptions and violence, that they over-stressed the role of perceptual/psychological variables, and that their focus upon political violence demeaned the concept of revolutions. Against this, the psychological theorists could make three points in their defence. The first, which was in fact mentioned by Gurr,[43] related to the inferential status of the psychological component of the theories. Inferences of this kind were, he noted, not uncommon in the social or indeed the natural sciences, and the psychological explanations were open to refutation in the same way as any other explanations. Until they were refuted, there was no reason to treat them as invalid. A second point which could be made was that it was easy to criticize the psychological theorists on the grounds that some of their empirical work had suggested that perceptual/psychological variables were less important than had been hypothesized, but that this would not have been known unless the theorists had attempted to systematically investigate their models and try to weight the relative influence of particular variables. In this sense they had made a major contribution to the study of revolutions. Finally, it could be suggested that, no matter whether or not revolutions were equated with political violence, there was general agreement that revolutions involved such violence. By providing explanations of political violence, the psychological theorists had materially assisted the explanation of revolutions, even if this was only considered to relate to one component of them. If only these claims are accepted, it is apparent that the enterprise of the psychological theorists was, whatever the objections and difficulties, justified and worthwhile.

3 Economic Theories of Revolutions

The subjects of economics and politics were combined as political economy in the works of many of the great thinkers of the nineteenth century. However, in the later part of that period, the study of economic behaviour became largely divorced from that of social and political behaviour and, in the first part of the present century, economics advanced in isolation from the other social sciences. Economists approached the analysis of economic behaviour in terms of rational choice analysis: they specified a set of assumptions which provided for individual or collective actors to choose between alternatives upon the basis of the maximization of utilities, and formally derived propositions from these to explain choices between bundles of goods and services. It was considered, by sociologists and political scientists as well as some economists, that the assumptions necessary in order to posit individual rationality were less appropriate in the spheres of social or political life than in the context of choices between competing bundles of goods and services. The basis of this assertion was stated by Schumpeter[1] in that, while rationality played some part in economic life, 'the typical citizen drops down to a lower level of mental performance as soon as he enters the political field. He argues and analyses in such a way as he would readily recognise as infantile within the sphere of his real interests. He becomes a primitive again. His thinking becomes associative or affective.' Given this, the explanation of political behaviour was held to lie within the realms of sociological or psychological theorizing, and these perspectives informed most of the research into such behaviour, particularly that concerned with voting in the liberal democracies. Voting behaviour became viewed variously in terms of responses to primary or secondary groups' norms[2] or as reflecting affective bonds between electors and parties.[3] Neither of these explanations conveyed a very flattering portrait of the electorate or indeed of democracy in practice; governments were decided not by the choices of a majority of rational actors, but by the block votes of groups or the success of parties in creating favourable images in the minds of voters. This implied that democratic government had fallen considerably short of the standards expected by political theorists such as Mill[4] who had supported the adoption of this type of system, and this became a source of concern to some social scientists. These began to investigate the possibility that the sociological and psychological theories of voting were mistaken, and that voters could indeed behave as rational actors. Thus Downs,[5] in a pioneering study, demonstrated how the formal economic model of consumers exercising rational choices could be applied to the analysis of electoral behaviour in a way that was consistent with the known characteristics of the electorate which had previously been held to militate against their making rational decisions. This work was extended by others, among them Olson,[6] both in the field of voting and in other areas of political choices, including revolutions.

The accounts of the three theorists who attempted to derive economic models of revolutions were all predicated upon the conventional assumptions for the application of such models in any sphere, namely that (1) individuals could always make a decision when confronted by alternatives; (2) the alternatives were ranked in order of preference; (3) preference rankings were transitive; (4) the individual always chose from among the possible alternatives that which ranked highest in his preference ordering (i.e. acted so as to maximize the differences between utilities and costs); and (5) s/he would always make the same choice when confronted by the same alternatives. Beyond these common assumptions, the theorists diverged somewhat in their approaches, reflecting their reliance upon different economic theories which were adapted to the case of revolutions.

IRELAND AND THE APPLICATION OF THE DOWNSIAN MODEL TO REVOLUTIONS

Ireland's[7] economic theory of revolutions was based on Downs's account of voting and party behaviour and he, like Downs, proceeded by making a series of strong assumptions to derive a simple model which was then progressively developed by the introduction of more realistic conditions. His initial case involved the assumptions that (1) participation on either side in a revolution was costless and (2) the support of an individual for one side or the other would determine the outcome of the insurrection. Given this, the rational individual would decide what to do by comparing, over a given future period, the utility he would derive from successful revolution ($E(U_r)$) and that he would derive from the continuation of the existing regime ($E(U_0)$). In this case, the individual's choice would depend upon his expected utility differential,

(1) $E(U_r) - E(U_0)$

and if this was positive, he would support the revolutionaries, if it was negative he would back the status quo, and if it was equal he would not participate. This of course was analogous to an individual deciding whether to vote for one party or another or to abstain.

Voting, however, involved costs, as did participation in a revolution on either side. For his second case, Ireland abandoned the assumption of costlessness and introduced the cost imposed by the state for supporting the revolutionaries (C_r), the comparable cost imposed by revolutionaries for supporting the state (C_0) and the balance of indirect costs to family or property which could be imposed by either contender upon opponents ($\pm C_e$). Given this, the appropriate equation describing the factors upon which a decision would depend would be:

(2) $(E(U_r) - E(U_0)) - C_r(\text{or } C_0) \pm |C_e|$

In this variant, the outcome depended not only upon the magnitude and direction of the utility components, but also upon how this compared with costs. It may be noted that the permutations of these allow for the individual to favour a side which will benefit him less in utility than the other because the costs which could be imposed by the former were greater than the net utility benefit, for example where $E(U_r) > E(U_0)$ but, because of the state's control of the means of repression, this was less than $(C_r + IC_e)$.

The second initial assumption was that individuals were certain that their participation one way or the other would determine the outcome. Ireland recognized that this was unrealistic, although he noted that this might exceptionally be applicable to cases where the choice of a particular leader could sway the balance and cited the instance of France in 1958, where the success or otherwise of the coup depended upon whether or not De Gaulle agreed to move against the Fourth Republic. This assumption was dropped for the general case, and a term (p) introduced to represent the extent to which the individual felt that his participation would affect the outcome of the insurrection. The third equation was thus

(3) $\quad p(E(U_r) - E(U_0)) - C_r(\text{or } C_0) \pm |C_e|$

i.e. the individual would weight his utility function by the chances that his participation would make a difference, and then compare this with the costs of particular alternatives. Ireland suggested that, at this point, it was important to recognize a central difference between voting and choice in revolutions. Voting only involved one level of activity, casting a vote one way or the other; participation in revolutions could involve multiple levels of activities, varying from verbal support to carrying out assassinations, and each of these would have different impacts on terms of influencing the chances of revolution (persuasion might be less effective than terrorism and hence the value of p differs between levels) or costs (from a telling off for opining that one side or the other was preferable to a firing squad for terrorism). Individuals thus construct different equations for different levels of activities, and choose that which maximized the positive balance between utilities and costs.

One of the central problems with Downs's original economic model of voting was that the inclusion of a value to represent the effects of an individual's participation upon the outcome (in this case of an election) considerably undermined the potential explanatory power of the theory. Clearly, the chances of any single individual determining the result were miniscule and, if an individual multiplied his expected utility differential by a term for the effects of his participation, the resultant value would be so small as to be effectively always outweighed by the costs of voting, and hence no one would vote. Downs provided an ingenious, if perhaps dubious,[8] solution to this; Ireland, in dealing with a case where if anything the impact of the individual was more remote (and certainly more difficult to calculate), was forced to derive a similar justification for participation having a high value in order to sustain his model. This was accomplished by arguing that a revolution was akin to a run on a bank. If a few depositors withdrew their accounts, it made little difference if one more individual did the same; if many individuals simultaneously withdrew their funds, the effect of one more withdrawal was minimal; but if, at some point in between these, a marginal individual took out his money, this raised the chances that the bank would crash and would be followed by a flood of other depositors who sought to secure their assets. In the case of revolutions, the marginal individual made little difference to the chances of success where there were only a few revolutionaries, or where there was so many that the outcome was guaranteed; but at some intervening point, the accretion or non-accretion of one individual would tip the balance one way or the other and thence determine the outcome of the insurrection. Given this, as well as the additional assumption that all individuals realized the imminence of the hour of decision at the same time, Ireland could argue that they perceived that their participation could exert a significant effect on the outcome and hence that the p term in their equations would have a high and positive value. Thus, when the utility differential was weighted by p, the outcome would be significantly above zero, and the $p(E(U_r) - E(U_0))$ expression would be relevant to the making of the choice between alternatives. Thus Ireland managed to retain the utilities within his equation and preserve the integrity of his model.

He then went on to suggest how, given this, revolutionary parties attempted to further the chances of revolution. The obvious strategy for them to adopt was to (1) raise individuals' values of their own participation to a high level (i.e. induce any given individual to feel that he was the marginal one who could determine the success or failure of the insurrection) and (2) maximize the expected utility differential from successful revolution (providing for greater expected utility from revolution than from maintaining the status quo) while minimizing the costs imposed by the regime upon dissidents compared to those imposed by the revolutionary party upon regime supporters. Ireland noted that the first objective could be assisted by the employment of mercenaries, of professional soldiers who could mount a challenge to the regime and push the insurrection nearer to the point at which it was poised one way or the other; the attainment of the second one could, he thought, be enhanced by side-payments (rewards accruing specifically to individuals active on the revolutionary side), which would provide an additional incentive (whether an immediate one in the form of cash or a future one of a position in the post-revolutionary hierarchy) to individuals to support the revolutionary option; additionally, costs of supporting the regime could be increased by harassing opponents, suggesting that high costs would be imposed if the revolution succeeded, or by a calculated programme of the destruction of the property of opponents or terrorism against their families. It was, of course, open to the existing regime to compete in the same ways.

If the revolutionary movement was more successful than the regime, i.e. it has physically survived, mobilized support through inducing a positive utility differential and a widespread perception that individuals' participation was critical to the outcome, and where it was unlikely that the goals of the revolution could be met by peaceful means, there would be a 'revolutionary situation'. This, Ireland argued, would continue up to the point at which, for a given individual, the costs of participation began to exceed the utilities to be gained from further participation. This could be because the existing regime initiated extreme repression or, if the regime was dismissed, the individual came to regard his continued participation as unnecessary to secure the revolution. Thus Ireland considered himself to have explained not only the circumstances under which revolutions would start, but also those under which revolution would end, and this completed his economic model of the revolutionary process.

TULLOCK, SILVER AND THE APPLICATION OF THE OLSON MODEL TO REVOLUTIONS

The other economic theorists, Tullock[9] and Silver,[10] based their accounts of revolutions on the work of Olson,[11] who had been concerned to demonstrate that, in given circumstances, participation in collective action could logically only be explained in terms of private, rather than public motives. Tullock considered that the application of this thesis in the context of revolutions was of fundamental importance in reorientating the study of revolutions along a new path: he concluded his article with the claim that 'Revolution is the subject of an elaborate and voluminous literature and, if I am right, almost all of this literature is wrong'.[12] This contention was based upon the appreciation that research on revolutions had stressed that individuals participated in them to further the lot of humankind, and Tullock's apparent demonstration that, even under assumptions entirely favourable to such an interpretation, it was the hope of private gain which motivated individuals to support revolutionary parties. He commenced by making the simplifying assumptions that the hypothetical state of Ruritania 'is governed by a vicious, corrupt and inefficient government. A group of pure-hearted revolutionaries are currently attempting to overthrow the government, and we know with absolute certainty that if they are successful they will establish a good, clean and beneficial government.'[13] What, asked Tullock, should an individual Ruritanian do about this matter? Three courses of action were open to him: to join with the revolutionaries, to support the existing regime, or to remain inactive. The potential pay-offs from these courses of action were labelled P_r, P_d and P_{in} respectively. The pay-off from inaction was specified as the product of two components, P_g (the benefit from an improved government, which Tullock argued was a public good in that it would be available to all following the revolution) and L_v, the overall likelihood of revolutionary victory. The benefit from doing nothing was thus,

(1) $\quad P_{in} = P_g L_v$

the increase in the provision of public goods multiplied by the chance of receiving them. The pay-off from becoming a revolutionary was held to be determined by the increased likelihood of revolution if the individual joined the revolutionaries (L_i), the private benefits from this course of action (such as high political office or status or wealth following the revolution which were only available to the individual and which were represented by R_i), the private costs imposed if the revolution was unsuccessful (P_i), the probability of injury in the course of revolutionary duties (L_w), the various types of injuries which might be suffered (I_r), and the entertainment value of revolutionary activity (E). These were related to the pay-off by the equation

(2) $P_r = P_g(L_v + L_i) + R_i(L_v + L_i) - P_i(1 - (L_v + L_i)) - L_w I_r + E$

In this, the various benefits were multiplied by the overall chances of revolution plus the difference to this made by the participation of the individual; the disbenefits were multiplied by the chances that the revolution would fail despite the participation of the individual, and the balance of these was offset against the negative factor of likelihood of injuries and the positive one of fun value. The third pay-off, that from supporting the regime, used some of the previously-defined terms as well as D_i to stand for the private rewards expected from the state for support and P_p as the costs imposed upon regime supporters in the event of successful revolution, and was held to be represented by the equation

(3) $P_d = P_g(L_v - L_i) + D_i(1 - (L_v - L_i)) - P_p(L_v - L_i) - L_w I_r + E$

Here, the benefits accruing from the continuation of the status quo were weighted by the chances of revolution minus the difference made by the individual's participation on the side of the existing regime; the disbenefits were discounted by the likelihood that the revolution would succeed even though the individual had opted for the regime, and the net produce of these was adjusted to take into account the injury and entertainment value terms as in the previous equation.

Tullock argued that a rational individual, having constructed these equations, would then compare them in order to derive the net benefit from participating on either side as opposed to remaining inactive. He would thus subtract P_{in} from P_r to define the benefits of supporting the revolutionaries, G_r, and would find the benefits of supporting the regime by taking P_{in} from P_d to give G_d. The effect of this operation was to remove the $P_g L_v$ terms from both equations, i.e.

(4) $\quad G_r = P_r - P_{in}$
$\quad\quad\quad = P_r - P_g L_v$
$\quad\quad\quad = P_g L_i + R_i(L_v + L_i) - P_i(1 - (L_v + L_i)) - L_w I_r + E$

(5) $\quad G_d = P_d - P_{in}$
$\quad\quad\quad = P_d - P_g L_v$
$\quad\quad\quad = D_i(1 - (L_v - L_i)) - P_g L_i - P_p(L_v - L_i) - L_w I_r + E$

It will be noted that the removal of one term involving P_g left only one other term including this in the equations, $P_g L_i$. However, Tullock argued that the chances of any single individual exerting an impact upon the success or otherwise of the revolution were so small that the L_i term could be treated to all intents and purposes as zero. If equations (4) and (5) were amended to take account of this, the remaining term involving a public good component dropped out of the equation (if L_i was zero then P_g multiplied by L_i was also zero, as were other terms involving L_i), and the final equations were:

(6) $\quad G_r = R_i L_v - P_i(1 - L_v) - L_w I_r + E$

(7) $\quad G_d = D_i(1 - L_v) - P_p L_v - L_w I_r + E$

Thus, for any individual, the choice between supporting the existing regime or the revolutionaries was determined by the balance of the private benefits and costs discounted by the probabilities of revolutionary success or failure minus the chances of various types of injuries but plus the fun value of participating in the revolution. This result had, of course, implications for the objectives of regimes and revolutionary movements. It was clearly irrational for them to attempt to appeal for support on the basis of increasing the supply of public goods: this term did not enter into the equations of individuals. Instead, each should seek to win support by competing in the provision of private rewards and in seeking to minimize the costs of such support while maximizing the costs of opposition. Thus existing regimes should offer high rewards to individuals for their adherence (particularly to induce members of the revolutionary movement or its elite to change sides and provide information[14]) and repress opposition effectively: revolutionary movements should counter this by bidding higher in the rewards stakes (particularly for informers and turncoats), intimidate the security forces of the regime and ensure that other regime supporters were severely punished. Given this, it would appear that revolutions occurred when, for some or all non-elites in society, the new balance of private benefits and costs was in the favour of the revolutionaries and this reflected the relative success of the revolutionary movement in competing with the regime in the provision of such benefits and protecting supporters/repressing opponents.

This analysis was, as noted earlier, in sharp contrast to Tullock's perception that research on revolutions had stressed 'public goods' motives, and he felt moved to explain why a 'paradox of revolutions' of this kind had emerged. Tullock suggested two main reasons for this. Firstly, many revolutions had been described by those who had taken part in them, and it was hardly to be expected that they would objectively explain their participation in terms of hopes of private gain. Ex-revolutionaries would stress public goods motives to present themselves in the best light, which Tullock conceded was 'quite human behaviour'.[15] The second reason was the bias of academics. Most of these, he suggested, would be interested in revolutions because of the public goods which had allegedly flowed from them. Given this, and the fact that no contemporary data was available to correct impressions, social scientists and historians would naturally tend to infer that, because they considered improved public goods had followed revolutions, these had been made with public goods motives in mind. However, his equations suggested that much of the work on revolutions needed to be rewritten to establish the various private motives/costs involved in support for the revolutionary movements which had challenged existing regimes.

The most notable attempt to utilize Tullock's theory was by Silver, who used the private benefits/costs model to derive a typology of the causes of revolutions, to explain the composition of revolutionary elites and to account for the aftermath of revolutions. Silver defined revolution as 'a period in which the frequency of revolutionary acts was extraordinarily high', a revolutionary act constituting 'an extra-legal act (violent or non-violent) intended by the actor to secure a change in governmental personnel, structure or policy'.[16] The causes of revolutions, he argued, could be modelled using the equations derived by Tullock, with two amendments. Whereas Tullock's 'E' term had stood for the entertainment value of participation in revolutions, Silver used E to stand for the psychic income from revolution, under which he included the individual's sense of duty to class, country, democratic institutions, the law, race, humanity or God, as well as his taste for conspiracy, violence and adventure. Silver also added a new term to the equation, V, which stood for the value of the time and other resources which the individual devoted to the revolution, and which had a negative value. The basic equation used by Silver was

$$(8) \quad G_r = R_i L_v - P_i(1 - L_v) - L_w I_r + E - V$$

which was the same as equation (6) above with the addition of the V factor. He then proceeded to demonstrate how this equation could be adapted to some of the apparently known facts to yield a fourfold classification of the causes of revolutions.

The first type of revolutionary causation was that which stemmed from political reforms. Silver alluded to the observations of De Tocqueville and others concerning the extent to which revolutions tended to follow limited reforms in societies previously distinguished by oppression, and noted that explanations of this had been cast in primarily psychological terms (as outlined in Chapter 2). He suggested that this explanation would, if recast in terms of equation (8), account for revolution as a rise in G_r following an increase in the value of the E term, E in this case standing for the psychic satisfaction arising from the alleviating of frustration and aggression. Silver rejected this proposition as dubious, although without giving a reason, and put forward an alternative interpretation. Reforms, he argued, effectively raised the chances of the success of the revolution as (1) they were perceived as an indication of regime weakness and (2) they resulted in benefits for the revolutionaries (by giving them parliamentary seats, media coverage, access to finance) which could be used as resources against the regime. This meant that the value of the L_v terms in the equation increased, and this implied that the magnitude of the private benefits component $(R_i L_v)$ rose while that of the costs of revolutionary failure $(-P_i(1 - L_v))$ fell; additionally, a greater chance of success was held to reduce the probability of injury. Thus reform increased rewards and decreased costs, with the consequence of a higher net benefit from supporting the revolutionaries, and this change motivated support for the latter to the extent that there was a serious challenge to the regime. Silver suggested that this analysis could variously describe some or all of the causes of the Belgian revolution of 1789, Jacobin conspiracies in Vienna and Hungary in 1794, the Prussian revolution of 1848, the Russian Revolution of 1918, the Polish and Hungarian revolutions of 1956 and the Black revolution in the United States in the 1960s.

The second cause related to defeat in war, and examples were held to include the English revolutions of 1204–68 and 1450–87 (following defeat at the hands of the French), the defeat of Napoleon which ushered in revolutions in France, Belgium, Poland, Spain, Italy and Portugal between 1875 and 1930, the Paris Commune in 1871 (following defeat of the French by the Prussians), as well as defeats preceding revolutions between 1917 and 1919 in Russia, Hungary, Germany and Turkey. In these cases, the effect of defeat in war was to demonstrate the weaknesses of the regime, with the consequence that the chances of revolution being successful improved, and this affected the private benefits term in equations positively while reducing costs and led to a greater net balance of gain from supporting the revolutionaries.

The third category of causations involved revolutions started by regime alienation of powerful individuals. Silver suggested that where a regime did not defend, or attacked, individuals such as local notables, the owners of large firms, major landowners, religious leaders or senior officers, this raised the personal return that these would achieve from successful revolution and led them to invest resources in support for opposition to the regime. Interventions of this kind were often in the form of palace revolutions, coups d'etat, insurrections, putschs, or fascist revolutions, and the example given was the 1955 revolt against Peron in Argentina.

The final causal pattern identified was revolutions initiated by widespread increases in hostility towards the regime which arose from either increases in group solidarity which followed government action detrimental to the group (a tax increase which discriminated against one section of the population) or a realization of group consciousness consequent upon the introduction of new ideologies or religions or a growth in affluence. The effect of these was to increase the psychic satisfaction derived from revolutionary activity (E), and this was held to increase the extent of participation and raise the chances of successful revolution. This change in the value of L_v in the equation influenced the magnitude of the cost and benefit terms which promoted a rise in G_r and stimulated support for revolution. Examples of this were held to be the Boxer revolution in China, the American revolution, and the growth of Black Power in the United States.

With the general causes of revolutions thus established in terms of the modified Tullock equation, Silver turned to the question of the composition of revolutionary elites, and the aftermath of revolution. Silver dismissed the explanation of revolutionary elites in terms of psychological motives or sociological characteristics virtually out of hand: a revolutionary was someone who had made a specific occupational choice – to become a ruler – and who was prepared to devote personal resources to revolutionary ends for this private motive. This, he suggested, could account for some of the known characteristics of revolutionary leaders. The latter came disproportionately from the young, which was unsurprising as the expected benefits from revolution would increase with the anticipated lifespan of an individual, and be greater for younger than for older people. Similarly, revolutionaries tended to be highly educated, which Silver interpreted in terms of the expectation that the more educated would occupy the dominant roles in a society following successful revolution, in which case the pay-off to them would be greater. Thus both youth and education would result in a higher valuation of the private benefits of revolution (R_i), and this explained the disproportionate presence of these characteristics among revolutionary leaderships. Silver also considered that the contention that the latter were motivated by private gains could be used to suggest why revolutions rarely resulted in fundamental changes, why they became routinized and differed from the society which preceded them only in so far as a new elite held power. This, he argued, was consistent with the fact that revolutionaries only wanted power and, once this was achieved, there was no benefit to them from radical social restructuring. In this sense, revolutions were no more than the jockeying of revolutionary careerists for place, position and power.

ECONOMIC THEORIES OF REVOLUTION – SOME CRITICISMS

These models were open to several criticisms relating to the ways in which they were specified and to the general validity of the economic approach to revolutions. Firstly, it may be pointed out that the conclusions of the economic theorists only applied to particular stages of revolutions, not to the revolutionary process as a whole, because of the assumptions made. Ireland specified this in equation (3) that the rational individual would discount his expected utility differential by the difference that his participation would make to the overall chances of successful revolution. However, this was only significantly non-zero at the point at which all individuals learned simultaneously that revolution was imminent and perceived that they could be the marginal individual whose participation would decide the outcome of the insurrection. Aside from the inherent implausibility of this particular case, it was apparent that, before or after this juncture, the utility differential was zero as the effect of participation term was zero, and choices would be made solely upon a basis of costs. Thus the conclusion that utility differentials played a part in the calculus of decision-making was only applicable at this point in the revolutionary process. This, incidentally, created difficulties in trying to use Ireland's analysis to suggest why anyone should create a revolutionary movement in the first place. Given that the discounted utility differential was zero, and that the existing regime could impose costs upon the individual far in excess of his ability to retaliate, it would seem unlikely that any rational individual would opt for revolution at all.

Tullock and Silver's models were predicated on the assumptions that there was a group of pure-hearted revolutionaries and that all members of the society were aware of their existence and certain that they would increase the supply of public goods. The assumptions of the presence of a revolutionary nucleus and that it appealed for support on the grounds of increasing the supply of public goods were necessary in order for individuals to have choices between alternatives and for public goods terms to enter into their equations. Additionally, there was an implicit assumption that the likelihood of revolutionary victory was significantly above zero, otherwise the L_v term could not have entered into the calculus. In real-world terms, Tullock and Silver were effectively taking it for granted that there was a revolutionary movement which (1) was well known to individuals, (2) had been successful in its ideological appeals to the extent of convincing the population that public goods benefits would definitely accrue from revolution, and (3) had mobilized enough support to create a real potential for revolution. Thus their analysis only related to the circumstances of individual choice at an advanced stage of the revolutionary process. It can be shown that, outside of this particular case (or the other limiting case where both L_i and L_v were equal to zero),[17] individuals would in fact have to take public benefits into account when computing the equations necessary to make rational choices. Suppose, for example, that individual Ruritanians were certain that a revolution would improve the supply of public goods, but there was no revolutionary movement in existence (L_v was equal to zero). Any given individual would be aware that for revolution to be possible a revolutionary movement was necessary, and that he could himself provide a focus for the creation of such a movement (L_i was non-zero). In this case, which could be held to characterize the early days of revolutions, the appropriate equation for the pay-off from participation would be

(9) $\quad P = P_r L_i + R_i L_i - P_i(1 - L_i) - L_w I_r + E - V$

and this would be equal to G_r, the net pay-off from becoming a revolutionary (as $L_v = 0$ by assumption and hence $P_g L_v = P_{in} = 0$). Here, the public goods term was retained in the equation. If, further on in the revolutionary process, there was some positive likelihood of victory, but the individual still felt he could play a part (i.e. both L_i and L_v were non-zero), the appropriate equation would be

(10) $\quad G_r = P_g L_i + R_i(L_v + L_i) - P_i(1 - (L_v + L_i)) - L_w I_r + E - V$

Again, a public goods term was present in the final equation. Thus, the private benefits conclusion was contingent upon the selection of a particular case, and could not be generally applied to the revolutionary process as a whole.

This limitation of the thesis that only private benefits would enter into the equation of individuals' private benefits was helpful in resolving a paradox between Tullock and Silver's analysis and the real world. If the outcome of individual decisions in revolutions was purely a matter of private benefits and costs, it would be entirely irrational for revolutionary parties to devote resources to winning support on the basis of increasing the supply of public goods (even if they succeeded in convincing everyone that successful revolution would increase the supply of such goods they would not benefit because this factor did not enter into the equations of individuals) or for regimes to try and 'buy off' revolution by reforms (as these similarly would not affect the equations of people making rational choices). However, revolutionary parties have placed great stress upon improvements in public goods in their ideologies, and regimes, as Silver noted in his discussion of political reform as a cause of revolutions, have attempted to modify their policies and avoid overthrow. This apparent paradox could reflect the fact that regimes and revolutionaries were not rational actors, which Tullock and Silver nowhere admit, or it could reflect the fact that competition over the supply of public goods was important at stages of revolution prior to that considered by these theorists. If this latter point is accepted, it has implications for Silver's analysis of the composition of revolutionary elites and of the alleged failure of revolutionaries to implement significant changes following their assumption of power. His comments concerning the private motives of revolutionaries would only apply to those joining when the revolution was under way; those who had joined prior to this would have done so in part for public goods motives. This opens up the possibility that the youth and education levels of revolutionary elites (in so far as the latter comprised early joiners) were amenable to explanation in terms of the greater concern of youth with public goods (youthful idealism) and the greater degree of exposure to ideas critical of the existing supply of such goods and to ways of improving this among the highly educated. Further, assuming that the revolutionary elite after a successful revolution included many leaders who joined before the chances of revolution became high, it could be argued that attempts at social transformation would be made. It seems difficult to deny that the revolutions in (say) France, Russia, China and Cuba were accompanied by attempts at fundamental change (the institution of a secular society based on liberty, equality, fraternity in France, war communism in Russia and China, economic and educational initiatives in Cuba), and these seem consistent with the thesis that revolutionaries had some public goods motives for making revolutions. The attempts at change may not be regarded as successful, but failure can be attributed to factors other than elite contentment with private benefits. Thus, for example, in the case of the Russian Revolution it could be argued that the need to increase economic output rapidly and respond to a hostile international environment (where expected proletarian uprisings in other countries had either not materialized or been defeated) was as much, or more, a factor in causing the failure of reforms as the satisfaction of the desires of the Bolsheviks by the achievement of power.

The models of Tullock and Silver were also open to criticism on the grounds of the concept of rationality employed in them. Downs,[18] in his original application of economic theories to voting behaviour, was careful to distinguish between two concepts of rationality. Rationality in one sense could be defined in terms of individuals behaving in accordance with a rationally-determined hierarchy of goals and opting for that alternative which maximized the chances of achieving a particular goal relative to others. However, Downs noted that it was not possible to construct general rules determining the rationality of the orderings of the ultimate ends to which individuals aimed (as such an exercise would necessarily involve interpersonal comparisons of utilities which it was not possible to make). This effectively rendered rationality in this sense as tautological. The rational individual was held to act in accordance with rationally-ordered goals, the irrational one either did not act in accordance with such goals or had irrationally-ordered goals. However, it could not be generally determined whether goals were rationally ordered, and hence whether the individual was behaving rationally or not. Therefore, any assertion that individuals acted rationally had to be based upon the assumption that individuals employed rational means to further rationally-determined ends, i.e. constituted a proposition that individuals behaved rationally because it was assumed that they behaved rationally. At the behavioural level, a given behaviour could be said to be rational only because it was assumed that, if this behaviour had been selected by the individual, it must have represented the best strategy of implementing rationally-determined goals otherwise the individual would have selected a different behaviour from the available alternatives. Thus Downs argued that rationality in this sense was tautological, trivial and empirically non-falsifiable. For these reasons, economists had opted for a narrower concept of rationality, that of making choices between alternatives so as to maximize the likelihood of achieving a given goal. This avoided unwarranted assumptions about the rationality of goals, defined rationality other than by assumption (the individual was required to opt for the best alternative to achieve goals given the utilities/costs involved), and was empirically falsifiable (an individual could be shown to be irrational if he did not select the best alternative available to him). Downs argued that, if rational choice models were to have any meaning, they had to refer to rationality defined in this way.

It is apparent that, while Ireland's economic model was based in a concept of rationality defined narrowly (with individuals exercising choice as to whether the status quo or revolution would yield the greatest net utility over the next period), the models of Tullock and Silver embodied the wider definition. In addition to the goal of selecting the existing or a revolutionary regime, individuals were portrayed as concerned with the other goals of having fun or achieving psychic satisfactions. They were required in the equation to choose not just between alternative means of attaining a given goal, but between goals themselves: for example, an individual who preferred the regime given the balance of utilities and costs had to offset the realization of this goal against the fun value of the thrills and spills of revolutionary life and/or the psychic well-being derived from fulfilment of his sense of duty to God, class, the law, democratic principles, etc. While a given individual might have been able to weight these goals relative to each other (and exercise *personal* rationality in choosing between them) there was no objective way of determining the rationality or otherwise of goal rankings (there were no general means of determining, for example, that the rational man should prefer fun value over net utility from the regime). Hence Tullock and Silver's contention that actors behaved rationally had to be based upon the assumption that goals were rationally-ordered and that the individual had selected the best means of implementing goals, i.e. that actors were rational because they were assumed to be rational. With respect to any given behaviour, say a decision to support the revolutionaries, the attribution that this was rational depended only upon the assertion that the behaviour must have represented the optimum strategy of implementing rationally-ordered goals otherwise the individual would have opted for another alternative, i.e. supporting the regime or inaction. Thus Tullock and Silver's models suffered from the problems inherent in the wider definition of rationality, and their specification of individual rationality in making choices between regimes and revolutionaries was based in a tautology and could not be falsified by reference to particular cases of behaviour. Further, they were not 'true' economic models in the sense that the latter related only to rationality conceived of in a narrow sense. In order to rescue Tullock and Silver from these criticisms, it would be necessary to drop the E terms from the equations, which would then only relate to the components of choices in relation to selecting the regime or the revolutionary option on the basis of maximizing the pay-off over the next period.

There is another implication of the restriction of economic models to one kind of rationality, which has some bearing upon their applicability to revolutions at all. If such models were concerned with the selection of means of attaining a single given end, then clearly they would only offer a total account of behaviours which were oriented towards a single goal. It is relatively easy to see how this would probably be the case in the context for which the theories were originally derived, that of a consumer choosing between bundles and services in a market. In this case individuals would be concerned to satisfy their immediate economic wants, and could reasonably be assumed to do this on the basis of choosing that bundle which, relative to others, maximized their net utility. However, as Plamenatz[19] has pointed out, the wants involved in choosing political parties in elections were more numerous as they covered the whole range of matters concerning the individual likely to be affected by which party was in power over the next period. In addition to economic wants, those relevant to the making of choices between parties would include non-economic wants, such as peace, stability or an alteration of the power structures of the society. Plamenatz argued that, given the multiplicity of goals which had to be included in electoral choices, and that the latter therefore were considerably affected by preferences between economic and a number of non-economic ends, the economic models concerned with means to a single end could not offer an adequate analysis of behaviour. Clearly, any argument of this kind would be even more valid in the context of revolutions than in that of voting behaviour. In the former case, the wants involved included all those relevant to the individual under the status quo as compared to a different type of society, and were likely to span almost the entire set of human wants in the economic, social, psychological, political and moral spheres. Thus the number and variety of ends which the individual would have to consider in choosing between regimes and revolutionaries would be very great indeed, and this would limit the scope of economic theories to explain behaviour even more than in the case of electoral choices.

ECONOMIC THEORIES OF REVOLUTIONS – CONCLUSIONS

Even if the two final points made above are ignored, it does not appear that the application of economic theories to revolutions was particularly helpful. Ireland's conclusion that the balance of utilities and costs was a factor in choices was only valid at one point in the revolutionary process (because of the need for individuals to discount utilities by the value of their participation), and this point was defined by somewhat improbable assumptions. Tullock and Silver's conclusion that only private benefits entered into the equations of individuals was found only to relate to individuals deciding when revolution was imminent and not to earlier points in the revolutionary process. Thus their models could possibly explain why membership of the Bolsheviks had increased dramatically in the closing months of 1917 or why many people joined the Nazi party in 1933; but no one has attempted to explain this other than as individuals jumping on a bandwagon at the last moment in the hope of private gains, and it is difficult to see any advantages in having this specified as a formal series of equations. In fact, Tullock and Silver's accounts were perhaps more interesting for what was revealed by amending their assumptions about the motives of those joining the revolutionary movement before it posed a real threat to the regime. It was suggested that there was a public goods component in the equations of individuals deciding who to support in this case: but this does not appear to have been taken into account in social science research into the motives of revolutionary leaders, despite Tullock's (unsubstantiated) assertion to the contrary. While explanations in terms of psychological or sociological deviance[20] abound, little importance has been accorded to the possibility that individuals may become revolutionaries because they believe that revolution will substantially increase the supply of public goods. It can thus be argued that Tullock and Silver's work was important for a reason opposite to that which they intended, i.e. as amended it highlighted the *absence* of consideration of public goods motives in the literature, not the predominance of these.

This potential insight is, however, contingent upon the economic models being both 'true' economic models and applicable to the explanation of behaviour in revolutions. However, these requirements appear to be contradictory. For the economic theories of revolutions to be proper economic models, they have to be formulated within a framework of the narrow conception of rationality (which was the case for Ireland's model but not for those of Tullock and Silver because of the presence of terms standing for different goals in their equations): but for the economic models to be adequate as explanations of choices in revolutions they had to include multiple goals, which implied that they had to be cast in terms of the broader conception of rationality. This, logically, would mean that while it was possible to derive an economic theory, or a theory of revolutions, the requirements for these could not be filled simultaneously to produce a genuine economic theory of revolutions.

4 Political Theories of Revolutions

Revolutions involve attempts to change the structures and institutions of the polity, the personnel of regimes, or the policies of governments: as such they constitute an inherently political phenomenon. The origins of the analysis of revolutions by political theorists can, depending upon the concept of revolution adopted, be traced variously to classical, or medieval, or early modern, political thought, as was noted in the Introduction. This 'first wave' of theories was concerned more with the normative aspects of revolutions – the ethics of revolt – than with the explanation of them, although causal models have been discerned in the work of some theorists, most notably Machiavelli.[1] He, of course, provided an analysis of the strategies and tactics necessary for political conspiracies to succeed in seizing power, based upon his experiences of political upheaval in the medieval Italian city states. The political conspiracy theory was, as Eckstein[2] has noted, extended by some of the 'second-wave' theorists to account for modern revolutions: thus, for example, the French Revolution had been explained as 'simply a successful political conspiracy by the Jacobins, based on efficient political organization'.[3] The study of revolutions was, on this basis, a branch of elite political history concerned with the description of the formation of conspiracies and of how these had succeeded in overthrowing established regimes. The 'third wave' of political theorists of revolutions were unlike their predecessors in two respects. In contrast with the normative theorists, they were only concerned to elicit the causes of revolutions: compared to the conspiracy theorists, they rejected the notion that revolutions were a matter of *haute politique*, and stressed that they had an essentially mass character and were rooted to a greater or lesser extent in mass feelings of deprivation or structurally-determined inequalities between groups in societies. This perception of the nature of revolutions was, of course, common to both the sociological and the psychological theorists who, as has been seen, posited various linkages between group interests, mass discontents and the occurrence of revolutions. The 'third wave' political theorists, however, contended that any relationships between these variables were mediated by, or only important in the context of the central political processes of societies, and that these processes had to be accorded a critical role if revolutions were to be explained adequately. Beyond this, the political theorists diverged in their approaches to revolutions, reflecting their adoption of different conceptual frameworks within which to consider this phenomenon, frameworks deriving respectively from the 'political functionalist' and 'political conflict' schools of thought. The former started from the proposition that polities could only be stable if there was substantive agreement among members as to the value and utility of the existing political system: in order to maintain such agreement, the components of the system had to fulfil a variety of functions, principally adapting to changes in the environment within which the system operated. If the system failed to meet these functional requirements, the consensus was broken, and dissident groups emerged who attempted to change the system and in the process created political disorder and instability. This could be countered by modifying the system, or if this was not possible, in the longer term by its reconstruction. Huntington[4] used this framework to analyze political stability and instability, the latter which included revolutions; his account was cased in terms of the degree to which political institutions could sustain consensus by meeting new functional requirements generated by economic and social modernization. The work of Tilly,[5] by way of contrast, stemmed from the 'political conflict' approach to the study of politics, where the polity was viewed as an arena within which groups competed for power, and through this wealth and status, and where the outcome of such competition was determined primarily by the balance of resources available to contending groups. Tilly attempted to derive a general model of group conflicts and a specific one of the determinants of the resources available to groups, and then used these to analyze the revolutionary forms of political conflict. Thus the political theorists of revolutions, like the sociological ones, offered accounts based in very different traditions of social scientific enquiry.

HUNTINGTON AND THE POLITICAL FUNCTIONALIST THEORY OF REVOLUTIONS

The genesis of Huntington's theory lay in an attempt to refute a crude theory relating economic and social modernization to political stability which was fashionable in American government circles in the 1950s and 1960s.[6] This commenced from the observation that the stable democracies were the wealthiest, the most industrialized, the most urbanized and the most educated societies in the world; the unstable polities were the poorest, the most agrarian, the most rural, and the least-educated societies. It was inferred from this that it was possible to create stable democracies in the developing nations by promoting what was variously described as 'economic development',[7] 'economic growth',[8] or 'modernization',[9] in order to provide the social and economic conditions which apparently sustained democracy in the West. In this way, the developing countries could be rescued from communism which, it was argued, bred in poverty and ignorance, and started along the path to American-style democracy. Thus – particularly during the 'Cold War' era – one of the central planks of American foreign policy was the promotion of modernization as a 'bulwark against international communism',[10] and large sums were dispensed in aid to developing countries thought to be at the point of industrial 'take-off' in order to hasten their economic development and consequent elevation to the status of stable democracies.

The work of Huntington, undertaken in the mid-1960s, derived from the contention that this policy had simply not worked. Statistics showed that, over the postwar period, there had been a dramatic increase in the incidence of political violence, disorder and instability, not least in those countries which had benefited under American or American-sponsored aid programmes. These data, he claimed, suggested that there were certainly no automatic links between economic and social modernization and political stability; indeed, in some cases it was possible to discern a relationship in the opposite direction, i.e. that modernization appeared to cause political instability. This point that the relationship between these variables was open to dispute was not, in itself, particularly original. Other social scientists, including Kornhauser,[11] Olson,[12] and Deutsch,[13] had all noted that modernization could create, as well as resolve, social conflicts by disrupting established bases of social solidarity, promoting bitterness among those groups which lost from economic development, and throwing up new social groups with interests opposed to those of dominant elites. It thus appeared that modernization could be associated both with political stability and instability, that there was no clear relationship between these variables. Huntington's original contribution was to suggest that this reflected a failure to consider the political dimensions of modernization, and to argue that, if political variables were included, it was possible to explain why, in some cases, economic and social modernization was associated with political stability while in others it appeared to induce political disorder. Thus the central concern of his work was to derive a theory which took full account of the political aspects and implications of modernization, and thence provided for an exposition of the linkages between the modernization process and the various political outcomes with which it was associated, including that of revolutions.

Huntington set out a general theoretical framework for his account in terms of a political functionalist approach to political stability. He started from the contention that the latter was a product of what he termed 'political community',[14] the degree to which there was a shared moral consensus in societies and a mutual interest among populations as to the maintenance of the existing order which was sustained over time. The extent of political community was, outside the limiting cases of total social harmony or total conflict, in part determined by the ability of political institutions – political organizations and procedures – to fulfil the functions of maintaining order, selecting authoritative leaders and resolving disputes. Such disputes stemmed from conflict between two or more 'social forces',[15] between economic, status, religious, ethnic or territorial groups in societies. The degree to which institutions were responsible for performing the functions necessary to sustain political community varied according to the type of society. In simple societies, conflict could be resolved by reference to traditional, ascriptive norms, and the role of political institutions was minimal; however, 'the more complex and heterogeneous the society . . . the more the achievement and maintenance of political community became dependent upon the workings of political institutions'.[16]

The ability of political institutions to create and sustain political community was the product of two factors: the scope of support for institutions, and the level of institutionalization. The former category related to the extent that institutions encompassed the population of the society. If only a small and unrepresentative section of society was included in its political organizations and procedures, the scope of political institutions was limited, as was its ability to fulfil the functions necessary for community; if, on the other hand, such institutions involved a large section of the population, their scope was wider, and they were more able to manage conflict by routinized means. The second variable concerned the extent to which organizations and procedures were stable over time and valued in themselves by the population, which reflected variously the extent to which they were: (1) capable or incapable of adapting to environmental change; (2) complex or simple in so far as any failure would involve the system as a whole or one of its parts; (3) aligned with major groups in societies or autonomous from them; (4) coherent or disunified; and (5) able to promote the public interest rather than the private ones of bureaucratic or conflict groups in societies. A lowly institutionalized society was one where institutions could not adapt easily, were relatively simple in structure, aligned with specific groups, non-coherent and unable to promote the public interest; a highly institutionalized society had the opposite characteristics.

Huntington then combined these various points to yield paradigms of 'traditional' and 'modern' polities. In traditional polities, the role of political institutions in creating political community was limited, the scope of political institutions was highly restricted and the degree of institutionalization was low. In a modern polity, political institutions were largely responsible for political community, participation was wide in scope and institutionalization was very high. Huntington argued that there was a necessary correspondence between these types of polities and stages of economic and social development. In simple, predominantly rural, agrarian societies where the economy was organized on the basis of self-sufficiency, conflict was predominantly between kinship, religious or racial groups, and its resolution was governed by ascriptive mores; the functional role of political institutions tended to be mainly that of providing for external defence. In consequence, political institutions tended to be of limited importance in the creation of political community, simple in structure, restricted in scope and low on institutionalization. In advanced, urbanized, industrial societies, conflict arose centrally from disputes over the allocation of economic and political resources between the major economic and social groups created through the highly-differentiated division of labour in a modern economy. Such disputes could not be managed by appeals to tradition, but had to be met by political institutions undertaking the additional functions of satisfying welfare and constitutional demands, to use Rostow's[17] categorization. Thus political institutions were critical to the maintenance of political community in such societies and, in order to sustain this role, were required to be complex (because of the range of functions), wide in scope (to incorporate lower-class groups in the polity), adaptable (capable of meeting welfare and constitutional demands), multiple (so that the failure of one institution to, say, implement a welfare demand did not compromise the entire political system), impartial (not seen to be a tool of a dominant class), coherent (united in order that division could not be exploited by one conflict group against another), and concerned to act in the public interest (as distinct from that of a particular class or status group).

The implication of this latter argument was that modernization had political, as well as social and economic components. Economically, modernization involved urbanization, industrialization and the expansion of education; socially, as Deutsch[18] had argued, it involved social mobilization, the breaking or eroding of older traditional commitments and their replacement by new ties and attitudes conducive to changing and expanding the productive capacities of individuals and groups in society. But, Huntington suggested, modernization also involved political changes, the changes necessary to develop from a traditional to a modern polity. Economic modernization and social mobilization created new groups and new demands and thence a need for political institutions to expand in scope and fulfil new functions, the latter involving increasing the level of institutionalization to that appropriate to a modern society. There was thus pressure for what Huntington termed *political modernization*;[19] he described the ability of existing institutions to modernize as their capacity for *political development*.[20] If these proceeded apace, i.e. the polity was able to incorporate new groups and political institutions were developed adequately, then political community could be sustained and modernization completed without political instability. If, on the other hand, actual political development lagged behind that necessary to implement political modernization, political institutions became unable to fulfil the functions necessary to maintain community, a process which Huntington called *political decay*.[21] The extent of such decay was measured as the *political gap*,[22] the distance between the actual scope of political institutions and the level of institutionalization and those necessary to maintain political community given economic modernization and social mobilization. The emergence of a significant gap implied a breakdown in political community, the emergence of groups which disagreed with the existing order and had an interest in changing it, and thence political instability. Huntington regarded the chances of modernization leading to stability or instability as being determined primarily by the speed of modernization. Economic modernization led to the disruption of traditional sources of social solidarity, the creation of new groups in society, and the raising of aspirations among populations. In order to maintain social and political stability, it was necessary to develop new sources of social solidarity, assimilate and integrate new strata, and meet aspirations. Where the modernization process took place over centuries, social and political systems had time to adjust; where, however, countries attempted to modernize in the space of only a few years, adjustment was impossible with the consequences that large sections of the population became alienated from existing social and political structures, new economic groups felt excluded from status and power hierarchies, and popular aspirations could not be met. Rapid modernization thus led to social frustration and demands on regimes which could not be accommodated: this motivated an expansion of political participation outside of established institutions in order to enforce demands, and thence political instability.

Such instability could take the form of coups (attempts to change leaders and policies), insurrections or rebellions (which also involved the reform of political institutions), wars of independence (struggles against the authority of an alien community), and revolutions. A revolution was defined as a 'rapid, fundamental, and violent domestic change in the dominant values and myths of a society, in its political institutions, social structure, leadership, and government activities and policies'.[23] Revolutions were thus distinguished from other forms of instability by the fact that they involved transformations of the dominant values and social structures of societies, as well as leaders, policies or institutions. Huntington noted that this was a highly restricted definition, and that it implied that revolutions were a 'historically-limited' and 'rare'[24] phenomenon. The examples he quoted were those of the 'Great' or 'social' revolutions, including the French, Chinese, Mexican, Russian and Cuban cases.

Three conditions were held to be associated with the particular outcome which occurred following the creation of a significant political gap in a society. The first was the extent to which modernization led to the joint social mobilization of key groups within the population. Huntington suggested that, in most societies, organized labour was integrated within existing structures, and the lumpenproletariat was innately conservative; this left the urban middle-class intelligentsia and the peasantry as the main potentially radical groups in society. He argued that, if economic modernization led only to the mobilization of the urban intelligentsia, riots, coups and revolts might follow, but not revolution; if the peasantry were not mobilized in modernization and remained loyal to the regime, revolution could not be effected. If, however, both of these groups were mobilized in the modernization process, i.e. there was *both* an urban and a rural basis for insurrection, this enhanced the chances of revolution. Whether this actually yielded a revolution depended in part upon the second factor, that these two groups should also have 'the capacity and the incentive to act along parallel, if not cooperative, lines'.[25] The chances of such an alliance depended upon (1) the success of revolutionary intellectuals in defining common ground between these diverse groups by the adoption of nationalistic appeals which transcended class differences, and (2) the extent to which there was visible reinforcement for such appeals in terms of the presence of colonial elites or alien groups in the country. If, because of the inadequacies of intellectuals and/or the lack of a foreign aggressor, a political coalition between the urban intelligentsia and the peasantry could not be created, these two groups tended to attack each other with the consequence of civil war but not revolution; the latter followed only upon joint, and effective, political action by these social forces. The third and final determinant of the outcome of modernization was differences in the capacities of polities to develop. Riots, coups or revolts were most likely to occur in political systems which had at least some longer-term capacity to 'expand their power and to broaden participation within the system': it was 'precisely this factor which makes revolutions unlikely in highly-institutionalized modern political systems – constitutional or communist – which are what they are simply because they have developed the procedures for assimilating new groups and elites desiring to participate in politics'.[26] Revolutions were only likely where institutions had no capacity to respond, or were only capable of limited responses, to the need for political development. Huntington suggested that highly traditional regimes 'headed by an absolute monarch or dominated by a landowning aristocracy' were unable to develop at all, and that a limited and inadequate ability to change was characteristic of both 'indigenous governments that have absorbed some modern and middle class elements and . . . are led by new men with the ruthlessness, if not the political skill to hang on to power' and 'colonial regimes in which the wealth and power of a metropolitan country gives the local government a seemingly overwhelming superiority in all the conventional manifestations of military authority and force'.[27]

These conditions, then, defined the circumstances under which rapid modernization would lead to revolution. Huntington considered that these involved three elements: an explosion of political participation outside of established institutions, the destruction of those institutions and the creation of new ones. While these elements were present in all revolutions, the order in which they occurred was held to vary systematically in accordance with two distinct patterns, which were termed the Western and Eastern styles of revolution respectively. The difference between these stemmed from Huntington's division between institutions which had no ability to develop, and those with a limited, if inadequate, capacity to change. In the former case, which comprised highly traditional monarchical or aristocratic regimes, he argued that the imbalance between existing institutions and those necessary for a modern society was so great that it became evident even to institutional incumbents that political decay was too far advanced to be rectified, and they effectively allowed the political institutions of society to collapse without major pressure from rebellious groups. Huntington quoted Pettee,[28] to the effect that, in this pattern 'The revolution does not begin with the attack of a powerful new force upon the state. It begins simply with a sudden recognition by almost all the passive and active membership that the state no longer exists': there is thus a vacuum of authority and 'Revolutionists enter the limelight, not like men on horseback, as victorious conspirators appearing in the forum, but like fearful children, exploring an empty house, not sure that it is empty.' However, the collapse of political institutions in this way did not guarantee a revolutionary outcome in the sense of a social transformation: in the ensuing struggle for power, urban radicals had to effect a political coalition with the peasantry, otherwise they would be defeated by conservative or moderate groups who would forestall social revolution. Huntington gave a number of examples of cases where an *ancien* regime had collapsed through advanced political decay, but urban groups had been unable to gain rural support with the consequence that non-radical groups had succeeded in consolidating themselves in power: these included France in 1830 and 1848, the aftermaths of the downfalls of the Habsburg, Hohenzollern, Ottoman and Qajar dynasties and the demise of the Syngman Rhee regime in Korea in 1960. Where, however, urban and rural forces were allied, there was an explosion of political participation beginning in the cities (where political institutions were physically situated and thus where the power struggle began) and spreading to the countryside in which the radicals were swept into power and then began to implement the changes necessary for the creation of a modern society. Huntington termed this the Western pattern or style of revolution, and identified it as present in the French, Russian and Mexican revolutions, as well as the first stage of the Chinese one.

Eastern-style revolutions occurred in colonial regimes or those which had only the capacity to absorb some middle-class elements, i.e. where political institutions had some ability to develop, but not to the extent necessary for full political modernity. Here, Huntington argued, development was initially adequate to contain urban social forces, but did not provide for the incorporation of the peasantry and their demands within the polity. In consequence there was an explosion of political participation in the rural areas, and a protracted war in which guerilla armies gradually encircled the cities. The failure of the regime to develop political institutions to a modern form eventually stimulated urban discontent, and following the formation of a political coalition between urban and rural groups, rural revolt was complemented by urban uprising and the regime was defeated. Political institutions were destroyed, and radical groups began the process of radical social transformation. Huntington suggested that this model of revolution applied to the later phases of the Chinese revolution, the Vietnamese revolution, and other successful anti-colonial revolts.

Thus Huntington synthesized theories of economic modernization, social mobilization and political functionalism to produce a new theory of revolutions. This is summarized in Figure 4.1. Revolutions occurred when rapid economic modernization resulted in the joint social mobilization of the urban intelligentsia and the peasantry which combined in an effective political coalition and either seized power following the collapse of completely decayed political institutions (Western-style revolutions) or successfully defeated a regime with institutions which had developed only partially to political modernity (Eastern-style revolutions). Rapid modernization accompanied by any other combination of factors was associated with political instability, but of a sub-revolutionary type, and gradual modernization was held to promote political stability.

	Social mobilization	*Efficacy of coalitions*	*Capacity of institutions for development*	*Outcome*
Rapid economic modernization	Urban intelligentsia and peasantry	Effective	None	Western-style revolution
			Partial	Eastern-style revolution
	Urban intelligentsia only	Ineffective	Adequate	Sub-revolutionary instability
Slow economic modernization				Political stability

FIGURE 4.1 *Huntington's theory of revolutions*

There are conflicting views as to the empirical validity of Huntington's theory. Gillis[29] suggested that the model of Western-style revolutions – where political decay induced institutional collapse followed by a power struggle in which conservative, moderate or (for a revolution) radical groups eventually emerged victorious – offered a good explanation of two modernizing revolutions in Europe, the French Revolution of 1789 and the Prussian one of 1848. In these cases, Gillis argued, social-structural models were of little use because they assumed that institutions were swept away by mass revolt whereas the pattern in France and Prussia was that such revolt had followed, not preceded, institutional collapse. Huntington's exposition of advanced decay as the cause of such collapse in rapidly modernizing countries fitted this pattern well. Further, his analysis of the nature of power struggles was helpful in explaining why, in France, modernization had been accompanied by social revolution, whereas in Prussia it had not (which, incidentally, implied that Gillis should not have described Prussia as a revolution on Huntington's definition of the term). In the former, the power struggle had been won by urban radicals who, with the support of much of the peasantry, had implemented a fundamental transformation; in the latter, the urban radicals had been unable to effect a coalition with the peasantry, and were defeated by conservative–moderate forces who had thus prevented an extreme outcome. Thus, in the context of these revolutions, it appeared that Huntington's theory had considerable explanatory value.

However, Tilly[30] and Russell[31] have claimed that there was a poor fit between the theory and other cases of political instability and revolutions. Tilly pointed out that Huntington's theory received very little support from Gurr's major empirical study of the causes of civil strife during the 1960s in a large sample of countries, most of which were in the process of modernization. Gurr, it will be recalled, quantified a number of independent variables and the dependent variable of civil strife and used regression analysis to assess the relative importance of each of the former in explaining the latter. The independent variables included a measure of the level of institutionalization. This proved to have a negligible ability to account for civil strife, whether this was conceived of in absolute terms (institutionalization explained only 1 per cent of the variance in civil strife) or relative ones (the social and structural facilitation variable, for example, accounted for nearly half of the variance in strife). Tilly claimed that this finding largely invalidated Huntington's theory, given the central role accorded in this to the level of institutionalization as the determinant of the form of political instability resulting from rapid economic modernization. Additionally, Tilly was by no means convinced that such modernization necessarily led to political instability at all. He suggested that the evidence for this provided by Huntington and others[32] related to too short a time period to adequately assess the relationship between these variables, and noted that the major study of trends over the longer term – that by Sorokin[33] – had failed to identify a clear positive correlation between the rate of modernization and political stability or instability. Further, Tilly[34] cited two examples of what he claimed was a negative relationship between the speed of modernization and political instability. Thus in France, increasing urbanization after 1830 had been associated with a reduction, rather than an increase in political violence; in 1848 the first European country to revolt was Sicily, one of the most slowly-modernizing nations, not one of the countries which was modernizing rapidly. On this basis Tilly argued that it was certainly not axiomatic that rapid modernization promoted instability, and hence that this component of Huntington's thesis was wrong.

Russell's objection to Huntington's theory was based upon its apparent inapplicability to modernization in South Africa during the 1950s and early 1960s. During that period South Africa modernized rapidly, and this impacted both on urban and rural groups; revolutionary leaders were available, there was a nationalist ideology to unite socially-mobilized groups and this was reinforced strongly by the visible target of a dominant elite of alien origin; political institutions were manifestly incapable of developing to incorporate new groups into the polity or catering for their demands; the level of political community was low as the black majority did not accept the dominant values of white supremacy or support political institutions designed to maintain that supremacy. On all of Huntington's criteria, there should have been significant political instability or indeed revolution: but South Africa modernized without political instability. Thus,

Russell suggested, the South African case constituted an empirical refutation of Huntington's theory.

It was possible that this apparent disagreement between Gillis on the one hand and Tilly and Russell on the other as to the validity of Huntington's theory was a reflection of the differences between the cases taken in so far as these fulfilled, or did not fulfil, the conditions necessary for the successful application of functionalist-type models. Huntington's thesis, like that of Johnson discussed earlier, was predicated upon the assumption that political stability could only be maintained if there was a high level of voluntary agreement among members of society as to the goals of society and the appropriateness of existing institutions to achieve those goals. Given that the attainment of such political community was contingent upon the performance of various functions by political institutions, the central condition for political stability was that such institutions were adequate to fulfil these functions successfully. The corollary of these propositions was that political instability was caused by a loss of political community occasioned by the inability of political institutions to perform functions, which Huntington ascribed to the total or partial incapacity of decayed institutions to develop and respond to pressures for modernization caused by social mobilization consequent upon rapid modernization. However, as was pointed out in criticism of Johnson's theory, this approach did not allow for political stability to be maintained, despite a loss of political community (or a low level of such community), by regime oppression or repression. Where regimes were united, willing and able to oppress and repress their subject populations, they could prevent or counter the emergence of challengers, and thence sustain political stability. This point, in the context of the relationship between modernization and political stability or instability, would suggest that this was mediated by regime capacities for oppression and coercion, as well, or instead of, the capacity of political institutions to develop. Clearly, where regimes had little or no control over coercive or repressive resources, they would depend entirely upon maintaining political community for survival; if institutions were decayed and wholly unable to maintain political community in the face of modernization or could only partially develop in response to pressures for political modernization, then Western- or Eastern-style revolutions would follow if modernization and social mobilization effected a critical coalition between key groups in society. If, however, regimes could control coercive or repressive resources, they could try to maintain political stability by this means despite a loss of political community stemming from institutional decay in the face of modernization. The success of this enterprise would depend upon whether coercion and oppression were effective in maintaining stability either while political institutions were given time to develop (in which case political authority on the basis of political community would be restored) or without such development (whereby authority would be based permanently upon force). If oppression and repression proved inadequate because of elite disunity, unwillingness or inability to counter insurgents, political instability would result; where elites were unified, prepared and able to maintain themselves by force, the country would be politically stable.

This analysis suggests that Huntington's theory was only applicable to cases where regimes had little or no capacity to coerce and oppress, but of dubious relevance where this condition was not met because no allowance was made for political stability to be maintained by oppression and coercion. It can be argued that this distinction underlay the divergent views as to the utility of his theory noted earlier. In both the French Revolution and the Prussian so-called revolution studied by Gillis, *ancien regimes* were deprived of control of the means of oppression and coercion by external war or loss of support among strata in possession of such resources. The authority of these regimes depended solely upon maintaining political community and, as suggested by Huntington, political decay precipitated institutional collapse and revolution. Most of the countries studied by Gurr, however, had military or military-backed regimes, which implied that they had a degree of control over coercive and oppressive resources. In these cases the chances of modernization leading to political instability were a function of the extent to which such resources were deployed effectively, not the capacities of political institutions for development. This interpretation is consistent with the lack of a relationship of any magnitude between the level of institutionalization and civil strife noted earlier; it is also reinforced by Gurr's other findings that facilitation and, to a lesser extent, coercive potential, were important variables in explaining such strife. The extent to which challengers were able to obtain facilities was, in large measure, determined by the effectiveness of regime oppression; indeed, the latter can be defined as attempts to deny facilities to opponents. Coercive potential, of course, related to the capacity of regimes to repress subject populations. Thus, in the sample of countries taken by Gurr, Huntington's model was of very limited relevance because it did not take account of oppressive and repressive variables. Finally, in the South African case cited by Russell, the white elite was united in agreeing with the use of force to maintain its dominance, willing to go to the extremes of organizing society in order to deny facilities to challengers (for example, by forcibly redistributing the population so as to minimize the opportunities for the initiation of large-scale collective violence, planning townships so as to contain and isolate revolts, and killing, imprisoning or exiling opponents so as to prevent the emergence of potential leaders of revolution) and repress gatherings with any potential to become a focus for violence (as at Sharpeville in 1961 where peaceful protestors were shot), and able to oppress and repress effectively through a completely loyal and well-equipped military. In this case, the extent of political community and the state of political institutions was irrelevant to political stability, and Huntington's theory was wholly inapplicable.

If this interpretation is correct, it may have implications as to the explanatory value of Huntington's model in explaining revolutions occurring in different time periods. Gillis's examples were of eighteenth- and nineteenth-century European revolutions, while those of Gurr related to civil strife in the second half of the twentieth century. It is at least arguable that, over this period, the capacity of regimes to oppress and to coerce has increased with the development of the study of counter-insurgency (i.e. regimes have learned from previous revolutions how to avoid this by denying facilities to challengers or repressing opposition) and improvements in military technology. If this is true, it would appear that Huntington's theory was most applicable to the older revolutions, where the conditions necessary to employ functionalist models were likely to be met, and least applicable to recent revolutions, where the chances of modernization leading to revolution were determined more by the factors of oppression/facilitation or coercive potential/repression. Thus Huntington's theory may be of greater value to researchers concerned with the earlier revolutions than those analyzing recent or contemporary ones. The latter may be more amenable to explanation in terms of a political conflict approach of the kind advanced by Tilly.

TILLY AND THE POLITICAL CONFLICT APPROACH TO REVOLUTIONS

The image of revolutions conveyed by the social systems model and the socio-psychological theories was one of the failure of systems/regimes to adapt or meet expectations generating frustration and psychic tension, which eventually reached such levels that individuals were involuntarily motivated to participate in spontaneous mass cathartic violence against the government which caused its downfall. The starting point of Tilly's analysis of revolutions was that this 'pressure cooker' image was at odds with the findings of those social historians who had studied the older revolutions at the grass-roots level, i.e. examined the available documentary data relating to individuals and small groups and attempted, on this basis, to reconstruct the sources and nature of revolutionary activity. Such studies had found that, prior to the revolution, there had been a marked growth of political organizations among deprived groups in the population: protests by such organizations had been met by attempts to suppress or repress them by established regimes; subsequent to this, new political organizations had sought to gain political power and used violence as a tactical and strategical weapon to achieve this objective. Revolutions were thus held to involve organized, voluntary and purposive political violence by deprived groups with grievances against governments. Tilly adduced support for this contention as applied to the modern world from Gurr's study of civil strife in a large number of countries during the 1960s. This, Tilly held, indicated that facilitation (which included the organizational and other resources available to revolutionary movements), coercive potential (regime attempts to repress new political organizations), and deprivation stemming from the lack of political power (which Tilly saw as directly relating to political violence rather than indirectly through psychological processes as inferred by Gurr), were the critical factors in explaining strife. Thus he argued that the social systems and psychological theories were based in an incorrect understanding of the nature of revolutions: what was required was a theory which took full account of the power, deprivational, organizational and coercive dimensions of the revolutionary process. While Huntington had advanced some way along this path by stressing the role of political factors – in particular the exclusion of new groups by an established political system – his account had been marred both by the stress upon the rate of modernization as a factor causing instability and the adoption of a functionalist approach which, as suggested in the previous section, severely compromised the validity and the applicability of his theory. Thus Tilly saw his task as the development of a political theory of revolutions which was consistent with historical and contemporary findings as to the nature of revolutions, independent of the rate of modernization, and based in a political conflict approach which allowed full consideration of the explanatory role of oppression/facilitation and coercion/repression.

The conceptual framework for this was specified by what Tilly[35] called his 'policy model'. Within any given population there was a government, defined as the organization 'which controls the principal concentrated means of coercion',[36] and there were groups trying to influence the government by the application of collective resources. These groups were 'contenders for power',[37] and could be divided into two classes: those groups which regularly and routinely claimed a response from the agents of the government, and those which were not, as a matter of course, seen as entitled to such a response. The former were contender members of the polity; the latter were contender non-members or challengers for political power. Given this, Tilly suggested that, at any given time, there were three different sets of interactions taking place within a population, namely: (1) members of the polity would be trying to apply resources to influence the government; (2) members of the polity would be testing each other through means such as elections and debates; and (3) challengers would be attempting to influence the government and acquire membership of the polity while members (acting largely through the agencies of the government) would be resisting this intrusion. Over any particular period of time, there would thus be conflicts between government and member contenders, different member contenders, and the latter and challengers, in which, Tilly claimed, some contenders would be successful in achieving political power while others would fail.

Tilly then analyzed the determinants of the performance of power contenders over time in terms of a 'mobilization model'. The ability of groups to achieve power was a function of the extent to which they collectively controlled normative resources (the commitments of members of the population to other members of the group, the group itself, and its ideals), coercive resources (means of punishing other men and limiting the alternatives available to them), and utilitarian resources (other resources especially those which men found it rewarding to acquire). Such resources were necessary if the group was to be able to indulge effectively in 'collective action', i.e. 'action in the pursuit of shared interests'[38] against the government or other contenders. Where a group increased its control over any or all of these three resources, it was said to be *mobilizing* and acquiring an enhanced potential for collective action; where its control was decreased, it was in process of *demobilization* and had a lower capacity for collective action. The capacity of groups to mobilize was determined by three factors: their existing stock of resources, the extent to which the environment was conducive to the acquisition of further resources (which depended upon whether society's stock of resources not held by the group was large or small and how much competition there was from other contenders) and, most critically, the organizational structure of the group. Where this was communal, i.e. group structures were small, localized and undifferentiated, groups were likely to invoke considerable loyalty but be unable to deploy commitment and organize on a large scale; where this was associational, i.e. structures were large, extensive and complex, groups would have less commitment but the capacity to organize effectively on a scale. Tilly suggested that this latter dimension was reflected in characteristic patterns of collective action between groups, with communal groups acting in an unco-ordinated, localized way, and associational groups initiating planned, disciplined and large-scale collective action.

The polity and mobilization models were then combined to yield a typology of forms of collective action which had led to violence. The first form was that of competitive action, whereby members of one group defined another as a rival and mobilized to attack its resources. Tilly considered that this form of action characterized conflict whereby one group attempted to gain resources from another in the same polity, and distinguished between the primitive version of this kind of collective action which was indulged by communal groups and the interest group version of associational groups. The second form was reactive collective action, by which groups whose resources were claimed by others responded to protect their position. This was held to be the mode of action of contenders within the polity which were demobilizing, i.e. losing resources to governments, other contender members of the polity, or challengers. Again, this had variants for the two types of organizations, with reactive collective action by communal groups being reactionary, that of associational ones defensive. The final type was proactive collective action, whereby a group laid claim to resources for which it had previously been considered ineligible, and was resisted by at least one other group. This mode characterized contenders who were in the process of mobilizing and gaining access to the polity, and whose proactive action occasioned reactive collective action from groups whose resources were threatened. Proactive collective action by communal groups took the form of revitalization movements, the associational form was termed offensive.

These forms and group variants of collective action were associated with different modes of collective violence. Communal contenders undertaking competitive action would deploy primitive collective violence in the regularized modes of ceremonials, contacts in routine assemblies or games; such contenders in the reactive case would employ primitive, reactionary violence of the kind manifest in food riots, machine breaking, tax rebellions of pure guerilla warfare; communal contenders involved in proactive action would indulge in the (unspecified) type of violence characteristic of millenarian groups. Associational contenders would, if involved in competitive action, use the violence associated with interest groups, shows of organized strength such as parades; if they were engaged in reactive action, they would defend their interests by extensively organized violence in which older symbols were reactivated to bolster failing strength; if associational contenders were challenging with offensive proactive collective action, the form of violence would include displays of the fact that the contender met the conditions necessary for membership of the polity, attempts to coerce existing members of the polity and agents of the government, and concerted efforts to gain control of the actions of the government. Tilly noted that this categorization of types of collective violence had two central implications, that (1) unmobilized sections of the population had little involvement in such violence (as this was undertaken by the members of contending groups), and (2) the form of violence depended upon the relationship of the participants to the existing structures of power (the pattern differed between those who were members of the polity and those who were to a greater or lesser extent excluded).

The incidence of these modes of collective violence was held to have varied over time, at least in the West. In the early modern period, the central conflict in Europe had been over the establishment of the powerful nation state; this had been resisted by communal groups indulging in primitive, revitalization, and reactionary collective action and associated types of collective violence. This had proved unavailing in most countries, where power had been successfully transferred to the centre, which acquired control of the major means of coercion and thence the ability to contain localized collective violence which had declined in consequence. This decline had been accelerated after the creation of a centralized state by the impact of urbanization and industrialization which had greatly reduced or destroyed traditional communal groups and created new socio-economic religions, or territorial groups which were associational in their pattern of organizations. Such organizations included the jointstock company, the political party and the trade union. Thus these, rather than communal groups, became the vehicles for collective action, which in the modern world took the forms of interest group, defensive or offensive action, and the modes of collective violence with which these were linked. This change in the character of groups was also associated with another development, that of coalitions between contenders. While communal groups had little capacity to organize or sustain coalitions with other groups because of their localized and simplist nature, associational groups which were well organized at national level could effectively combine to attack the resources of others or defend their own stocks of such resources.

The new associational groups began, in the course of time, to mobilize resources and use these to attempt to influence the government and acquire membership of the polity: they thus initiated offensive proactive collective action, which stimulated defensive reactive collective action from potential loser contenders who were already members of the polity. Such conflict could lead to a variety of outcomes: among these was revolution.

Tilly suggested that, for an event to qualify as a revolution, it had to involve 'some minimum combination of (a) revolutionary situation and (b) revolutionary outcome'.[39] A revolutionary situation 'begins when a government previously under the control of a single, sovereign polity becomes the objective of competing, mutually exclusive claims on the part of two or more distinct polities. It ends when a single sovereign polity regains control over the government.'[40] The hallmark of a revolutionary situation was thus the appearance of multiple sovereignty where, within a given population, there were in effect two or more competing polities commanding the allegiances of different sections of the population and claiming the right to be the single, sovereign, polity. This conception of a revolutionary situation was similar to Amman's[41] analysis of revolutions as involving 'power blocks' clashing for control of the state, or Bell's[42] discussion of revolutions in terms of competition between two separate political systems, each competing to be the single authoritative allocator of values in the society. A revolutionary outcome comprised the displacement of one set of power-holders by another, i.e. a transfer of power between governments and/or polity members and contenders. Such power transfers could take forms varying from the replacement of the personnel of government through to the replacement of a previously dominant class by a new one: thus revolutionary outcomes could vary from a transfer of political power through a transfer of political, economic and social power.

Tilly commenced his explanation of revolutions by discussing the causes of the emergence of revolutionary situations. He identified, firstly, a longer-term cause, the inability of the government and polity members to incorporate new strata into the polity and provide adequate compensation for loser groups. While this was one cause of a revolutionary situation, it was not the only one: the occurrence of the latter also depended upon the presence of three factors which Tilly termed the proximate causes of revolutionary situations. The first cause was the appearance of contenders, or coalitions of contenders, advancing exclusive alternative claims to control over the government currently exerted by members of the polity. Such contenders could either be groups which from their inception had been committed to the fundamental transformation of the structures of power (the origins of which, Tilly suggested, were little understood), or groups which had previously operated within the rules of the polity but who had been unsuccessful in gaining membership (as with new associational groups) or in preserving control over resources (loser groups within the polity). The emergence of the latter types of contenders reflected the inability of governments to resolve conflict which stimulated groups to reject the existing polity and to try and create a new one within which demands could be met. The second proximate cause of a revolutionary situation was the development of commitment to the claims of these contenders by a significant section of the subject population, particularly where this was activated in the face of disapproval or prohibition by governments. Tilly suggested that two classes of government actions could lead to this outcome. One was where the government suddenly failed to meet specific obligations which members of the polity felt were well established and critical to their welfare. This factor, as Tilly noted, bore affinities to the 'J' curve theory of revolutions, whereby a sudden inability of the regime to meet popular expectations rapidly increased frustration to levels at which individuals were motivated to aggression against the regime. However, Tilly argued that the critical relationship between this and a revolutionary situation was not that the masses spontaneously revolted, but that frustration increased popular commitment to challengers, and hence the resources – including the ability to deploy aggression in the pursuit of tactical or strategic objectives – at their command. The other class of actions was where the government made a rapid or unexpected increase in its demands for resources from a subject population. Examples of this included rises in taxes, conscription, the commandeering of land, crops or farm animals or the imposition of corvées. Such demands increased commitment to groups challenging for entry to the polity (who were required to contribute without being allowed political or economic rights) or loser groups (whose dwindling stock of resources was further depleted by government confiscations). This, as with the previous class of government acts, enabled contenders to further mobilize.

Tilly noted that both of these classes of acts were often occasioned by war: defeat was a failure by governments to fulfil expectations and obligations, and wars often required governments to find new sources of monies in order to finance increased military expenditure. The third proximate cause of revolution was that the agents of the government had to be unable or unwilling to maintain the status quo of coercion, i.e. suppressing contenders or containing popular discontent and thus preventing the appearance of mobilized contenders. The absence of an ability to coerce could, Tilly suggested, be variously attributed to an insufficiency of the means of coercion, inefficiency in applying these means, or inhibitions as to the use of high levels of coercion. Tilly noted that involvement in external wars, particularly if a polity was on the losing side, often diminished the control of governments over the means of coercion and increased their vulnerability to attack.

These were the causes of a revolutionary situation: Tilly went on to examine the causes of revolutionary outcomes, the extent of power transfers following a revolutionary situation. His discussion related to two aspects of this, those factors causing any power transfer, i.e. a revolutionary victory at the end of the revolutionary situation, and those causing variations in the extent of power transfers following this. Revolutionary victories could be attributed to two causes, the first of which was whether or not challengers formed a coalition with a polity member or with polity members in the revolutionary situation. Such a coalition would increase the chances of success by, on the one hand, allowing challengers access to the resources of organized groups within the polity and creating opportunities for infiltration and subversion, and on the other depriving the polity of such resources. Tilly regarded this factor only as one increasing the likelihood of revolutionary victory: revolutionaries could win without a coalition, and the forming of a coalition did not guarantee that the revolutionaries would win. The factor which would guarantee this was if challengers or coalitions gained control of substantial force, of the balance of available coercive resources, and this was the second cause of a revolutionary outcome. Tilly suggested that the extent of such control was determined by the extent of military disloyalty to the government in the revolutionary situation, particularly in the early stages, and quoted Russell's[43] study to the effect that revolts in the present century had only been successful if some defections from the military to the revolutionaries had occurred in the initial phases of the revolutionary situation to support this contention.

Given a revolutionary victory, the next question related to the causes of variations in power transfers following the overthrow of the government. Tilly identified two causes of variations in revolutionary outcomes: the extent of the division between competing polities in a revolutionary situation and the extent to which the new revolutionary regime was formed by a single challenger or contender or a narrow or broad coalition of organized groups. With regard to the former, Tilly noted that the gulf between competing polities could vary from minimal to great, and he suggested that the larger the magnitude of this split, the greater the extent of power transfers following revolutionary victory as (a) the more all groups in society would be polarized between competing polities and the less likely it would be that a *modus vivendi* could be achieved in a post-revolutionary settlement (i.e. that agreement could be reached for polity members to continue holding positions of power); (b) the more experience the revolutionary movement would acquire in governing and the less it would need to rely upon older power-holders to keep the machinery of government in motion; and (c) the more opportunity and justification the revolutionary movement would have to attack existing power-holders and thus prevent their chances of retaining power. The second cause related to the composition of the new polity created following revolutionary victory. While coalitions in a revolutionary situation promoted the chances of such a victory and any revolutionary outcome at all, the extent of coalitions in new regimes was held to be inversely related to the degree of power transfer which took place: the broader the composition of the new regime, the more polity members would keep their existing power positions, and the less power would be transferred to new holders. Tilly considered that the realization of this prospect tended to precipitate the disintegration of challenger-member coalitions formed in the revolutionary situation following the overthrow of the old government, as challengers or polity members sought to defeat their former coalition partners and dominate the power hierarchies of the new regime. The extent of power transfer depended upon the outcome of this power struggle: where the new regime included a wide range of groups, i.e. where none had proved dominant in the power struggle, power transfers would be limited; these would be greater in proportion to the decline in the number of groups participating in the new polity and be most extensive where a single challenger emerged triumphant. In the last case, the magnitude of power transfer would be the same as if the revolution had been made by a single challenger without a coalition in the revolutionary situation and which had, upon victory, arrogated the positions of power to its own leaders and followers.

Tilly noted that these two causes of revolutionary outcomes could reinforce or offset each other in their joint effects upon the extent of power transfers. These effects would be reinforcing if both were in the same direction (for example, where a major split in the revolutionary situation and the presence of only a single challenger in the new regime jointly promoted extensive power transfer or a minimal degree of division between competing polities and a broad coalition in the new regime both acted to produce very limited power transfers) or offsetting if they were not (where a great divide in a revolutionary situation would be associated with a large power transfer but where the breadth of the membership of the new regime dictated a more limited one or where a low degree of division would suggest limited power transfer but a narrow-based new regime dictated more sweeping changes).

The two constructs of the extent of the split in the revolutionary situation and the extent of revolutionary outcomes (the former of which partially determined the latter) were then used to define a typology of revolutions. Tilly presented this by means of a Venn diagram, part of which is shown in Figure 4.2. The unshaded areas defined revolutions with 'pure' characteristics: full-scale revolutions were delineated by high degrees of division between competing polities in revolutionary situations and extensive power transfers, the latter being reinforced by the absence of coalition in the new regime created following revolutionary victory; in civil wars, moderate to high splits in revolutionary situations were accompanied by moderate to high degrees of power transfers, these revolutionary outcomes also reflecting the narrow to fairly broad basis of the revolutionary settlement; insurrection involved moderate to high splits in revolutionary situations, but the effect of these upon power transfers was diluted by the offsetting factor of a broad to very broad coalition forming

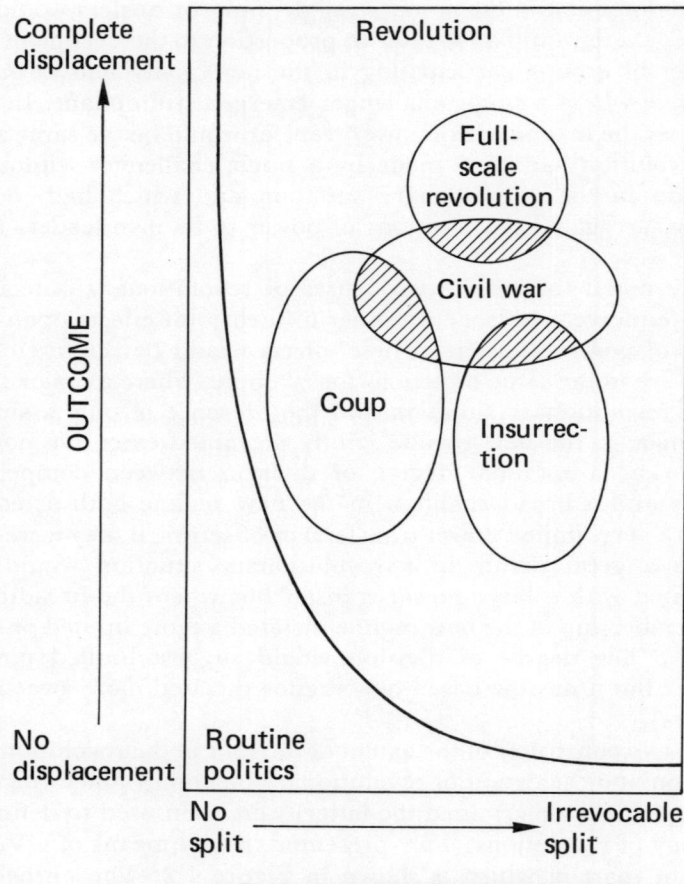

SOURCE: C. Tilly, *From Mobilization to Revolution* (Reading, Mass.: Addison Wesley, 1978) p. 198.

FIGURE 4.2 *Tilly's typology of revolutions*

the new regime and the extent of such transfers was only low to moderate; coups were defined as where low to moderate splits were associated with low to moderate power transfers, the levels of these being reinforced by the broad or very broad basis of the coalition in the revolutionary regime. The shaded areas represented overlaps between these types of revolutions: the lower end of the scale of power transfers in full-scale revolutions was similar in magnitude to that in the upper reaches of such transfers in civil wars, these reflecting respectively a wider and a narrow basis of new regimes than in 'pure' full-scale revolutions or civil wars, and these types of revolutions could not be distinguished from each other; similarly the upmost regions of the power transfers in insurrections involved transfers comparable to the lower end of the scale of those appropriate to civil wars, again reflecting patterns of coalition in new regimes (a somewhat narrower-based regime than was apparent in pure insurrections, a somewhat broader one than which typified pure civil wars) and revolutions of these kinds could be termed either insurrections or civil wars; finally, the upper limits of power transfers in coups were co-extensive with the lower limits of those associated with civil wars, as coalitions in new regimes in the former were more restricted than in 'pure' coups and coalitions in new regimes in the latter were wider than in 'pure' civil wars, and hence the two types of revolutions were not discrete within this range. Thus, while there were different patterns of revolutions, they merged into each other and became indistinguishable at the margins.

The final aspect of Tilly's work which may be mentioned is his analysis of the likelihood that revolutions would be followed by major social restructuring. He suggested that part of such restructuring was power transfers, and in this sense the extent of restructuring was the extent to which power had been transferred in a revolutionary outcome. Thus restructuring would scale from minimal in insurrections or coups to maximal levels in full-scale revolutions. But he also considered that the extent of power transfers would be related to restructuring in the wider sense of not only changing power-holders but the structures of power in themselves. Changes in the incumbency of a few power positions in the polity, as in many coups, would be unlikely to be accompanied by more than minimal attempts at reform; massive power transfers as in full revolutions would give new power-holders the opportunity to try and remodel social, economic and political structures. Tilly noted that it was difficult to assess the extent to which such restructuring was successful in the few historical cases of full revolutions, as the effectiveness of this could only be established over centuries rather than years or decades. However, the two centuries since the French Revolution did provide a long-enough period to allow the evaluation of restructuring. Tilly considered that, in this case, restructuring had been successful, as the revolutionaries had destroyed the juridical structure of feudalism, effected large transfers of wealth, subjugated the church, and provided a different basis for the development of French society in the nineteenth and twentieth centuries.

The main components of Tilly's theory may be summarized schematically. The causes of a revolutionary situation are set out in Figure 4.3. The causes of a revolutionary situation were thus (1) longer-term government inability to incorporate new associational groups or compensate losers and (2) the proximate causes of the appearance of challengers, increases in commitment to these, and loss of coercive control by the state. If the first condition was not met, the polity remained stable without undue coercion; if this was not, but the proximate causes of revolutionary situations were not present, governments were able to maintain themselves by coercion.

Longer-term cause	*Governments*	*Proximate causes*	*Outcome*
New associational groups demand entry to the polity and initiate offensive proactive collective action Potential loser polity members respond with defensive reactive collective action	Unable to incorporate new groups/ compensate losers	Appearance of challengers Government loss of means of coercion Unacceptable and sudden government failures/demands for new resources increases commitment to contenders	Revolutionary situation
		Any or all of above conditions absent	Political stability maintained by coercion
	Able to incorporate new groups/ compensate losers		Political stability

FIGURE 4.3   *Causes of a revolutionary situation*

	Whether or not coalition formed	Control of force	Whether any power transfer	Magnitude of power transfer
Revolutionary situation	No coalition	Challengers gained control of force	Revolutionary victory	Depended upon how far the effect of the split in the revolutionary situation was reinforced or offset by absence of coalition
		Challengers did not gain control of force	Defeat of the revolutionaries	—
	Coalition	Coalition gained control of force	Revolutionary victory	Depended upon how far the split in the revolutionary situation was reinforced or offset by pattern of coalition
		Coalition did not gain control of force	Defeat of the revolutionaries	

FIGURE 4.4 *Determinants of revolutionary outcomes*

The determinants of revolutionary outcomes may be summarized in Figure 4.4. The condition for any revolutionary outcome, i.e. the revolutionary victory necessary for any power transfer to occur, was that challengers or coalitions gained control of force: the chances of this, Tilly argued, were greater where challengers formed coalitions with polity members than where they did not, i.e. of the set of cases where no coalition was formed in the revolutionary situation, there would be proportionately fewer revolutionary victories than in the set of cases where a coalition was formed. Given a revolutionary victory, the magnitude of power transfers was determined jointly by the degree of split in the revolutionary situation and the pattern of coalition, which, depending on whether these factors reinforced or offset each other, gave rise to different types of revolutionary outcomes as detailed in Figure 4.5. Thus a moderate to high split in the revolutionary situation was associated with full-scale revolutions, civil wars and insurrections or combinations of these, the types depending upon the extent of coalition in the new regime. The extent of such coalition likewise determined whether the outcome of a low to moderate division in the revolutionary situation was a coup or a coup with a level of power transfer appropriate to civil war.

Extent of the split in the revolutionary situation	*Extent of coalition in new regime*	*Extent of power transfer*	*Type of revolution*
Moderate to high	None, very narrow	Massive	Full-scale revolution
	Narrow	Great	Full-scale revolution/ civil war
	Fairly broad	Moderate to high	Civil war
	Broad	Low	Civil war/ insurrection
	Very broad	Very low	Insurrection
Low to moderate	None, very narrow, narrow	Moderate to high	Coup/civil war
	Fairly broad, broad	Low	Coup

FIGURE 4.5 *Revolutionary situations, revolutionary outcomes and types of revolutions*

This theory is open to criticism on four grounds. Firstly, it can be argued that Tilly seemed to confuse the causes of revolutionary situations and revolutionary outcomes with these *events* themselves. The causes of a revolutionary situation were held to be the appearance of contenders, their mobilization of new popular commitment, and the government's loss of control of the means of coercion: but surely the state of multiple sovereignty which constituted a revolutionary situation was *defined* by these three factors, by contenders being able to mobilize and compete because the government could not prevent this by suppression or repression. The causes of a revolutionary situation were whatever variables explained why contenders had appeared, why substantial sectors of the population had transferred their allegiances to such contenders and why the government was deprived of coercive control. A similar point may be made with respect to Tilly's analysis of the cause of any revolutionary outcome, i.e. revolutionary victory. This was held to be caused by the acquisition of the balance of coercive resources, of control of force, by the revolutionaries: but it was the possession of such force which defined a revolutionary outcome in this sense, i.e. a revolutionary victory was the gaining of control of force by the revolutionaries. The causal factor was whatever explained why the revolutionaries had been able to win coercive resources and defeat the government. With respect to the magnitude of power transfers following revolutionary victory, Tilly claimed that this was jointly determined by the extent of division between the competing polities in the revolutionary situation (a genuine cause) and the composition of the new regime. However, the latter variable surely *was* the magnitude of power transfers: a narrowly-based new regime which included no or few members of the old polity defined a case of extensive power transfers or a broadly-based regime including a significant number of groups previously within the polity was a limited transfer of power. The causal variables were whatever determined the composition of the new regime which, as Tilly's typology of revolutions indicated, included the nature of revolutionary situations but others as well (for example, those which determined why a moderate to high split in the revolutionary situation lead to types of revolutions varying from insurrection to full-scale revolution).

These mis-specifications of causalities would be of little consequence if Tilly had explained why his so-called causes had occurred. But the second criticism which can be made of this theory is that it was deficient in explanatory variables not only where he mistook causes and defining conditions but also more generally. The longer-term cause of a revolutionary situation was held to be the government's inability to incorporate new associational groups within the polity and to compensate loser groups; but why some governments should be able to do this by routine politics while others could not was never explained. The first of the proximate causes of a revolutionary situation was the appearance of contenders. Tilly noted that, in the case of groups which were revolutionary from their inception, little was known of the factors promoting their origins. Other contenders comprised groups which had attempted to gain entry to the polity within the rules but which had been rejected and had turned to the revolutionary option. But Tilly did not try to account for why, in some cases, groups should be accepted by the polity while in others they should be rejected. He could of course suggest that this was contingent upon the government's ability to cope with conflict, upon the first long-term factor mentioned above. While this would seem to be the case, it is hardly helpful in the absence of any explanation of the causes of the latter factor. Tilly did comment upon the causes of the other two proximate variables, increases in popular commitment (caused by government failure to meet expectations/unacceptable impositions upon a subject population) and loss of coercive control (military defeat/demobilization) and noted that both of these were often associated with involvement in external wars. He also suggested a cause of revolutionary victory – military disloyalty particularly early in the revolutionary situation – but failed to explain the circumstances under which militaries would be loyal or disloyal or to what extent militaries might be disloyal. The magnitudes of power transfers in revolutionary situations were held to reflect in part the extent of division in the revolutionary situation; but Tilly did not explain why the degree of division should vary between cases. The other determinant of this was the composition of the new regime; but, while Tilly suggested that this depended upon the outcome of a power struggle between former coalition partners, he did not enlarge upon the causes of the emergence of a broad- or narrow-based coalition, except in so far as this was influenced by the degree of splits in the revolutionary situation, but this brings the argument back full-circle as he did not explain this variable in the first place.

Thirdly, it can be argued that, even where Tilly did specify true causes, the hypothesized relationships between these and revolution depended largely upon strong assumptions. Tilly admitted that one of his proximate causes of revolutionary situations, the growth of commitment among subject populations, was similar to some of the hypotheses advanced by the socio-psychological theorists, but he stated that the impact of this upon revolution was only through increasing the resources available to contenders. This would only be the case if all revolutionary violence was necessarily organized and directed, but this is not axiomatic. It could, for example, be plausibly argued that outbursts of mass, spontaneous violence (say the attack on the Bastille) were the signal to revolutionary groups that the time for an uprising was ripe, that mobilization was a realistic possibility, and that following this they harnessed violence to their own tactical and strategic purposes (the Jacobins organizing in the Paris sections). Tilly also suggested that such a growth of commitment and loss of coercive control by governments were frequently associated with external wars, particularly where regimes had lost. But, while there is an undoubted correlation between wars and revolutions, it is far from perfect; regimes have lost wars without losing control of the means of force or lost the control of coercive resources without wars having occurred. War would only lead to loss of control where regimes were seen as illegitimate, where they had failed to maintain political community; the hypothesized relationship between war and revolution thus depended upon the assertion of loss of regime legitimacy and, given that revolutions could happen without wars, it would seem likely that the general effect which Tilly identified was between regime legitimacy and revolutions with war as one factor promoting a decline in such legitimacy. These arguments both imply that the assumptions by which Tilly excluded socio-psychological or institutional variables from his analysis were invalid.

The fourth and last criticism which can be made of Tilly's theory is that it failed to validate the political conflict approach employed in his research by providing adequate alternative explanations to those stemming from socio-psychological or functionalist perspectives. It is perfectly possible to suggest explanations in these terms for some of the causes identified by

Tilly. Thus the long-term cause of revolutionary situations, the inability of governments to manage conflict, could be held to reflect the inability of political institutions to develop and incorporate the demands of new groups, as suggested by Huntington; the appearance of radicalized contenders who were previously acting within the rules of the polity can likewise be attributed to the failure of the institutions of the latter to develop; variations in the extent of divisions in revolutionary situations could be attributed to either the extent of cognitive dissonance or frustration among the masses (as suggested by Schwartz and Tanter and Midlarsky respectively) or to the varying adaptive capacities of political institutions (if these could develop to some extent prior to the revolution and provide some resources to groups, the gap in the revolutionary situation would be less than where such institutions had failed to develop at all and thus contenders required a much larger reallocation of resources); military disloyalty, the condition for a revolutionary victory, could be explained by institutional factors such as the extent to which the military fulfilled a wide range of functions within the polity or only a few technical specialized ones[44] or the abilities of institutions to generally maintain political community, militaries being less likely to be disloyal where regimes were regarded as legitimate than where they were not;[45] it could be argued that institutional forms were important in determining the composition of new revolutionary regimes as, if these were wholly decayed, the successful revolutionaries would have to create entirely new institutions, and man and shape them themselves, whereas if they were partially decayed revolutionaries could take them over but keep on the older experienced personnel of the old regime to maintain administrative continuity; finally, it could be suggested that the extent of institutional decay was related to the degree to which revolutions might lead to social transformations, in so far as a need to construct new institutions arising from total decay would be associated with radical changes as revolutionaries would be starting afresh completely, while partial decay would leave some institutions intact and lessen the extent of transformation. Tilly's account only offered assertions to counter these different interpretations (if polities were as described in the polity model, political institutions would only fulfil coercive functions and relate to revolutions in this way rather than in those described above, or if there was a link between relative deprivation and revolutions it was direct and not mediated by psychological processes) and these hardly constituted a substantive basis upon which to adjudge socio-psychological or institutional approaches as inappropriate to explaining revolutions.

If, however, Tilly failed to refute other modes of explaining revolutions, he did provide the basis for an alternative explanation of these in terms of conflict between organized groups and governments, the outcome of which depended upon struggles for the control of resources. Tilly thus derived an approach which set the findings of social historians and of Gurr (mentioned on pp. 80–1) into a more general context, and which could – at least with the addition of new explanatory variables and hypotheses relating these to revolutions – be used to explain a wider range of cases, especially the recent revolutions which Gurr's study suggested were more related to oppression/facilitation or coercion/repression than to institutionalization. The corollary of this last point was that Tilly's theory would be less applicable where the importance of these explanatory variables was reversed, as Gillis suggested was the case in the European revolutions in the first half of the nineteenth century, and this implied that even a reworked version of the theory within the original framework would only account for a sub-set of revolutions not the class of revolutions as a whole.

POLITICAL THEORIES OF REVOLUTIONS – CONCLUSION

Political theories of revolution came to be associated with conspiracy theories during the nineteenth century and the first half of the twentieth, reflecting an association which, as was suggested in the introduction to this chapter, can be traced to Machiavelli. The equation of the political approach with such simplist, elite-oriented and highly conservative (in the sense that the revolutionary masses were only regarded as the dupes of power-hungry conspirators and not as genuinely discontented) theories meant that political variables were neglected in accounts of revolution which favoured explanation in economic, social or psychological terms. The works of Huntington and Tilly were stimulated by theories of revolutions which took little or no account of political variables: the former's starting point was an attack upon a crude economic theory of the relationship between modernization and political stability, while Tilly took exception to both the social systems and the socio-psychological approach to revolutions. These theorists attempted, in different ways, to develop a new, complex, mass-orientated political approach to revolutions which took full account of the origins of these in deprivation and inequalities. Huntington cast his theory in terms of the relationship between economic modernization, social mobilization and the ability of political institutions to develop and maintain political community; Tilly examined revolutions from the perspective of groups conflicting over the allocation of resources. It was suggested that the political functionalist model of Huntington was inadequate as a general theory because it failed to give due weight to the ability of regimes to maintain themselves by coercion and oppression. The latter variables played a central role in Tilly's theory – for a revolutionary situation to develop or any revolutionary outcome to occur the government had to lose control of the means of coercion – but this theory was deficient in explanations at a number of points, and restricted in its application to cases where coercion and facilitation were critical factors to the exclusion of institutional or socio-psychological ones. But, if these theories were flawed, they also had considerable merits: both linked economic, social and political variables to produce multi-factorial accounts of revolutions (although this was more apparent in Huntington's theory than that of Tilly) and both did not simply try to analyze the causes of initial uprisings but went on to consider the development of revolutionary situations and revolutionary outcomes (the latter being analyzed more completely in Tilly's theory than in Huntington's). Further, to judge from the work of Gillis (motivated by that of Huntington) and Skocpol[46] (who acknowledged a debt to Tilly), the political theorists jointly succeeded in reinstating political variables among the variables held to be of importance in explaining revolutions. In these senses, Tilly and Huntington may be said to have made a contribution to the study of revolutions.

5 Social Science and Revolutions

The central question which the 'third wave' theorists sought to answer was 'why do revolutions occur?' The theorists clearly had very different conceptions of both what was to be explained and how the explanation should be approached. Johnson conceptualized revolutions in terms of the reconstitution of social systems, and explained them by reference to factors relating to the inability of such systems to fulfil the functions necessary to their survival and by the incidence of accelerators. Barrington Moore regarded revolutions as the replacement of previously-dominant classes by new ones (in bourgeois democratic and communist peasant revolutions) or the enforced transformation of lower classes by upper ones (fascist revolutions) and accounted for them in terms of patterns of exploitation, class relations and class coalitions. Skocpol focused upon social revolutions whereby one class supplanted another and remodelled society, and explained these in terms of the structural dynamics of class and class–state relationships in the domestic and international contexts. The socio-psychological theorists conceived of revolutions as illegal and politically-violent behaviours and viewed these in terms of psychological processes triggered by perceived deprivations, such processes being described in terms of cognitive dissonance by Geschwender and Schwartz and frustration-aggression by Davies, Tanter and Midlarsky, Bwy and Gurr. The economic theorists viewed revolutions as behaviours selected by individuals upon a rational basis and determined by the balance of discounted utilities and costs in the case of Ireland and the balance of discounted private benefits and costs in the theories of Tullock and Silver. Huntington considered revolutions to involve the reconstitution of political institutions and analyzed them in terms of the inability of such institutions to perform the functions necessary to maintain political community in the face of rapid modernization and social mobilization. Finally, Tilly defined revolutions as multiple sovereignty and power transfers and explained these in terms of organized groups mobilizing resources in the pursuit of political power. There was a multitude of apparently diverse answers to questions as to why revolutions occur.

This state of affairs could, on the one hand, be attributed to the fact that the study of revolutions is, inevitably, value-laden, and as such a range of theories reflecting different values or different combinations of values is all that could be expected. Revolutions are not naturally-defined phenomena comparable to those studied in the natural sciences and cannot be studied in a disinterested way. The form of a particular chemical or physical structure is determined by nature independently of scientists seeking to explain it; researchers, it is argued, do not bring their values to bear in proposing or evaluating explanations. Revolutions, however, are subjectively-defined phenomena, defined by those agents who research them; given that revolutions are a controversial subject, theorists are bound, consciously or unconsciously, to interpolate their own values in both defining revolutions and explaining them. Thus knowledge about revolutions must be inherently ideological. Theories of revolutions are ideological statements, and the multiplicity and diversity of the 'third wave' theories can be interpreted as a reflection of the different values, or value-combinations, of those social scientists who have studied revolutions. It could thus be argued, using Button's[1] typology of conservative, liberal and radical perspectives on political violence, that: the economic theories were a statement of the conservative perspective (revolutions were processes whereby revolutionaries motivated solely by personal gain seized power); the socio-psychological theories contained elements of this perspective (if revolutions were as defined above, only those activists who stood a chance of office in the new regime would benefit, thus mass action could not be rational and would reflect uncontrollable mass impulses of the kinds described as arising from frustration or cognitive dissonance); the functionalist theories of Johnson and Huntington could be described as embodying a liberal perspective (revolutions were processes by which institutions were reformed to make them compatible with a changing world, as where social systems had failed to adapt homeostatically or political institutions did not develop, these instances of institutional failure being rare and unusual); the conflict theories of Tilly, Barrington Moore and Skocpol were radical in perspective (revolutions were an extreme instance of endemic group conflicts in which progressive groups displaced older ones, such groups including territorial, religious, ethnic or class contenders in Tilly's model, classes in Barrington Moore's theory, and classes and states in Skocpol's account). This is not to say that the various theorists necessarily set out to produce conservative, liberal or radical theories of revolutions, but that their theorizing was inevitably contaminated by values and hence were essentially ideological in character. Wolin[2] has suggested that this implies that the social scientific theories were, in kind, no different from either the 'first wave' explicitly normative theories of revolutions or from revolutionary ideologies. The inference indicated from this is that the 'third wave' theories can be viewed as a set of additions to the ideologies of revolutions, as simply new statements of the conservative, liberal or radical perspectives on this phenomenon.

The multiplicity and diversity of theories of revolutions could, on the other hand, be interpreted in terms of the various theories being based upon an assumption about revolutions which was untrue. The 'third wave' theories were all predicated upon the belief that, if a set of events or processes could be designated as revolutions because they had common characteristics, they could then be explained by common causes specified in general causal statements. Dunn,[3] however, has questioned the veracity of this belief. He made a comparative survey of eight twentieth-century revolutions, those occurring in Mexico, Russia, China, Yugoslavia, Vietnam, Algeria, Turkey and Cuba, and concluded that, overall, the discrepancies between these 'are at least as striking as the uniformities' and the uniformities were 'on the whole more like lexical preconditions for applying the category "revolution" at all than . . . empirically-discovered attributes'.[4] This claim suggested that the only uniformities in revolutions were the characteristics that defined them as revolutions, but that the causes of such revolutions were unique to each case. Given this, it was evidently not possible to produce an adequate general causal theory of revolutions *per se*. If theories were not based on specific cases, they had to be tautological: if the only uniformities were the characteristics of revolutions, then such theories had necessarily to posit that the characteristics of revolutions were also the causes of revolutions, i.e. revolutions were explained by revolutions. There were certainly some examples of tautologies which were arguably consistent with this contention among the 'third wave' theories, most notably Tilly's confounding of the causes and characteristics of revolutionary situations and outcomes, Tullock and Silver's designation of revolutions in terms of rationally-chosen behaviours and explanation in such a way that behaviours could not be other than rational, or Johnson's confusion between the accelerators which were necessary and sufficient for revolutions and the characteristics of the revolutionary process itself. The other implication of Dunn's thesis was that, if tautology was to be avoided, theories of revolutions would have to be based upon specific cases; but, given that these were unique, clearly findings could not be generalized. It could be contended that an example of this was provided by the very different opinions of Gillis and Russell as to the utility of Huntington's theory of revolution. In the French Revolution taken by the former, there was some apparent fit between the causes of revolution and the 'political decay' model; in the South African case taken by the latter there was no fit in so far as the revolution projected in Huntington's theory had not occurred. This could be explained by the fact that Huntington's theory encapsulated the causes in one case, but not in the other which was quite different in its pattern of historical development. Thus it might be argued that Huntington's theory was useful in the French context, but that it was not, indeed could not, be regarded as a general theory. Thus theories of revolutions were tautological in so far as they were general and non-tautological in so far as they were specific, i.e. they could not be both non-tautological and general. In this sense, the plethora of social scientific theories of revolutions could be interpreted as reflecting methodological errors. It was easy to produce, and impossible by definition to test, tautologies, and thence multiple theories were only to be expected; similarly if social scientists were under the illusion that theories based in specific cases offered general theories it was not surprising that a wide range of theories had resulted, reflecting the different causes indicated by the different cases taken.

These interpretations would imply variously that the 'third wave' theories were either ideologies or misplaced pretensions to general theories, that the contribution of theorists to the understanding of revolutions was limited to either piling new ideologies upon an older stock of ideologies or, in a few cases, perhaps providing insights into the causes of particular revolutions although not revolutions in general. It is, however, possible to suggest a third interpretation of the theories of revolutions which lies between these extremes of evaluation, which would imply that the 'third wave' theorists of revolutions had made a more substantive contribution to the subject. Revolutions are subjectively-defined and explained phenomena, and as such the study of revolutions is an inherently-ideological exercise; but this does not mean to say that all theories of revolutions are equal in the extent to which they offer explanations for revolutions, or that all theorists of revolutions are equally motivated to produce favourable or unfavourable accounts of revolutions. While there may be no difference in kind between the work of active revolutionaries and social scientists studying revolutions, there is a difference of degree: the former seek to mobilize support and to justify revolutions, while the latter seek to explain them as a social and political phenomenon. Thus while both sets of theories have an ideological basis, they differ as to whether this is intended to promote specific political ends and thence in the extent to which explanation is a goal of theorizing. It can certainly be suggested that there were differences in the types of theories discussed in this book and revolutionary ideologies along these lines. While a reading of Paine, or Mao, or Lenin would leave no doubt as to the authors' predilections about revolutions, this is not, in general, the case with the social scientific theorists. Their theories can, as suggested earlier, be associated with particular political perspectives, but these associations were not usually consistent. Thus, for example, the socio-psychological theorists explained mass behaviour in terms of non-rational processes associated normally with a conservative perspective; but they also stressed that these had their origins in deprivations which could either be institutionally induced (as suggested by the liberal perspective) or structurally induced (as suggested by the radical one). Barrington Moore's account could be included under the radical perspective, but he himself denied this and in a later work[5] specifically dissociated himself from this in favour of an approach which could be described as liberal. Among the functionalist theorists, whose general perspective was held to be liberal, Johnson included non-rational mass action among the causes of revolutions (which is associated with the conservative perspective) and Huntington's model had a class-structural component in the analysis of class coalitions (which usually characterizes radical approaches). It can thus be argued that the social scientific theories did not embody at least clear and consistent political objectives in the same way as revolutionary ideologies; the theorists did not appear, in most cases, to be consistently supporting one ideological line or another, and their declared aims eschewed simply supporting the status quo in the world or changing or modifying it in favour of explaining it. Further, in pursuit of this objective, the social scientific theories were in most cases based upon, or associated with, bodies of historical and quantitative data in a way that is unusual, if not entirely foreign, in revolutionary ideologies. Thus it can be argued that the social scientific theories differed in degree of ideological motivations and explanatory content from pure revolutionary ideologies, even if both types of theories were in essence ideological. However, given the last caveat, it could be argued that the explanatory content of social scientific theories was irrelevant; such explanations could not embody objective knowledge, and hence it was inconsequential as to whether or not explanations were presented as the truth could never be ascertained any way. But, if revolutions are ideologically-defined phenomena, the only way in which they could be understood at all was by ideologically-loaded explanations. Therefore, short of abandoning the study of revolutions, it would appear that the greater the explanatory content of theories, the greater the extent to which revolutions could be explained. On this basis it can be suggested that the ideological nature of theories of revolutions did not necessarily imply that the 'third wave' theorists had to be written off as mere ideologists, that they also made a contribution to the explanation, and hence the understanding, of revolutions.

This would, of course, only be the case if there were common causes of revolutions for social scientists to explain, a proposition which, as has been seen, was questioned by Dunn. He cited a number of counter-examples, which he appeared to claim refuted, or could refute, general theories of revolutions. But, as MacIntyre[6] has argued, the ideological nature of knowledge about revolutions means that it cannot be known whether counter-examples to theories should lead to their rejection, the restriction of their scope or their amendment. A counter-example, or a set of counter-examples, could indicate that theories were wrong in the first place, that they had to be applied only in a given set of circumstances, or that they needed to be qualified by the invocation of auxiliary hypotheses if their generality was to be preserved. In order to decide between these alternatives, it was necessary to have objective knowledge of what made a theory true, false, true within limits, or capable of extension so as to be true. However, knowledge of revolutions was inherently ideological, and thence it was not possible to objectively distinguish the status of a counter-example with respect to a theory. Thus Dunn could only claim to have refuted general theories of revolutions by his counter-examples, and this claim is open to dispute, both in overall terms and with respect to the theories considered in this book. With respect to the overall status of his claim, it may be noted that other historians, including Brinton[7] and Wolf,[8] have both identified common causes of revolutions. With regard to the social scientific theories of revolutions, Dunn's analysis implied that general theories of revolutions had to be tautological; as was seen some had elements of tautology, but the vast majority presented genuine causal theories. It could be argued that this was only where they were based in, or applied to, single cases, as with Huntington's theory which appeared to be relevant to France, and such theories were not generalizable, as with the application of this theory to South Africa. But this counter-example need not necessarily invalidate the theory; rather it should indicate that its scope was restricted (it should only be applied in societies where regimes were unable or unwilling to use coercion effectively) or that it required extension (by including oppression/facilitation and coercion/repression variables). Further, it can be pointed out that Barrington Moore, Skocpol, Davies, Tanter and Midlarsky, Bwy and Gurr all produced theories which were applied over a set of cases, i.e. were apparently general, which were non-tautological, which would appear to indicate that there was no necessary association between the generality of theories and the extent to which they were tautological. Finally, it may be noted that alternative explanations of tautological theorizing or of the inability of theories to cope with counter-examples can be found. These could variously be attributed to poor theorizing, inadequate theorizing, or lack of research across a wide range of case studies.

It can thus be argued that the 'third wave' theories of revolutions did make a contribution to the understanding of revolutions, albeit in the form of ideological explanations of an ideologically-defined phenomenon, and that they did have some potential as general theories, albeit with the proviso that counter-examples reflected the need to improve theories rather than to reject them. If these contentions are accepted, it would also appear that the future of the study of revolutions need not be just the production of more ideological statements or more fallacious general theories, but would take the form of building up upon the foundations laid by the 'third wave' theorists. These provided both new explanations and flawed ones; clearly they created a basis for furthering the explanation of revolutions by the reworking and extending of their theories as well as attempting to evaluate hypotheses by new empirical research. The value of such new work may seem ultimately trivial, as objective knowledge cannot be attained and it is at least conceivable that general explanations might be inappropriate to revolutions; given this it could be argued that the results would not be worth the effort entailed. On the other hand, if knowledge of revolutions is to be furthered at all, it would appear to be necessary that social scientists continue to strive for objective knowledge even though this can only be ideological and try to produce general theories even though such theories could be predicated upon a methodological error. In this respect, theorists of revolutions are no different from social scientists studying any other subject, whose accounts are also necessarily ideological and who deal with phenomena as comparative without knowing that they necessarily can be compared. As such, theorists of revolutions face the same choice as social scientists generally; they must, as Mackenzie[9] has written, either attempt the impossible, or abdicate. Thus the way forward would appear to be in the consolidation and advancement of the theories of the 'third wave' theorists, if only because knowledge, however imperfect, is preferable to ignorance.

Notes and References

INTRODUCTION

1. Thus Copernicus's treatise on astronomy was entitled *De revolutionibus orbium coelestium*, 'of the revolutions of heavenly bodies'.
2. See Hatto, '"Revolution": An Enquiry Into the Usefulness of a Historical Term', pp. 502–3.
3. Elliott, 'Revolts in the Spanish Monarchy', p. 110.
4. Arendt, *On Revolution*, p. 43.
5. Kumar, *Revolution*, p. 17.
6. Paine, *The Rights of Man*, p. 166.
7. Arendt, op. cit., pp. 51–3.
8. There is a useful summary of Marx's theory in Cohen, *Theories of Revolution*, pp. 54–76.
9. Calvert, *Revolution*, pp. 16–20.
10. Davies (ed.), *When Men Revolt and Why*, pp. 85–6, Zagorin, 'Theories of Revolution in Contemporary Historiography', p. 23.
11. Silver, 'Political Revolutions and Repression', p. 67.
12. See Forster and Greene (eds), *Preconditions of Revolution in Early Modern Europe*, pp. 3–18.
13. Popper, *The Open Society and Its Enemies*, pp. 44–5, Bell, *Resistance and Revolution*, pp.17–18.
14. Kort, 'The Quantification of Aristotle's Theory of Revolution', pp. 486–93.
15. Zagorin, op. cit., p. 23.
16. See Bell, op. cit., pp. 22–3, Arendt, op. cit., pp. 35–9. For a more sceptical view see Crick's Introduction to *The Discourses*, p. 73.
17. Waltzer, *Revolution of the Saints*, p. 10 especially.
18. Arendt, op. cit., p. 23.
19. Barrington Moore, *Reflections on the Causes of Human Misery*, p. 23, Huntington, *Political Order*, p. 265.
20. Bell regards Locke as the first political theorist to comprehend revolution in anything like the modern sense of the term. See Bell, op. cit., pp. 24–7.
21. Freeman, *Burke and the Critique of Political Radicalism*.
22. De Tocqueville, *The Old Regime and the French Revolution*.
23. A comprehensive survey of Marxist thought is presented in D. McLellan, *Marxism After Marx*.
24. See e.g. Huntington, op. cit., pp. 3–4, 314, Leiden and Schmitt, *The Politics of Violence*, pp. 13–14, Greene, *Comparative Revolutionary Movements*, p. 6.
25. Sorokin, *The Sociology of Revolution*.
26. Le Bon, *The Psychology of Revolution*.

27. Edwards, *The Natural History of Revolutions*.
28. Pettee, *The Process of Revolution*.
29. Brinton, *The Anatomy of Revolution*.
30. Chorley, *Armies and the Art of Revolution*.
31. Brogan, *The Price of Revolution*.
32. Lasswell and Kaplan, *Power and Society*.
33. Gross, *The Seizure of Power in a Century of Revolutions*.
34. Ellwood, 'A Psychological Theory of Revolutions'.
35. Yoder, 'Current Definitions of Revolution'.
36. Riezler, 'On the Psychology of Modern Revolutions'.
37. Gottshalk, 'Causes of Revolution'.
38. Hatto, op. cit.
39. Neumann, 'The Structure and Strategy of Revolutions: 1848 and 1948'.
40. Hopper, 'The Revolutionary Process'.
41. Deutscher, 'The French Revolution and the Russian Revolution: Some Suggestive Analogies'.
42. Palmer, 'The World Revolution in the West'.
43. Wallace, 'Revitalization Movements'.
44. Freeman, 'Theories of Revolution', p. 339.
45. Eckstein, Introduction to Eckstein (ed.), *Internal Wars*, pp. 1–4.
46. Ibid., p. 4.
47. On the distinction between 'over-arching' and other kinds of theory, see Mackenzie, *Politics and Social Science*, pp. 81–110.
48. See Parsons, *The Social System*, and Parsons and Shils, *Towards a General Theory of Action: Theoretical Foundations for the Social Sciences*. An exposition and critique is contained in Gouldner, *The Coming Crisis of Western Sociology*.
49. Pye, 'The Roots of Insurgency and the Commencement of Rebellions', p. 162.
50. Of which the most notable example is Adorno *et al.*, *The Authoritarian Personality*.
51. See e.g. Bell, *The End of Ideology*, Lipset, *The First New Nation*, Almond and Verba, *The Civic Culture*.
52. See the summary in Olson, 'Rapid Growth as a Destabilizing Force', pp. 529–30.
53. The proceedings of which were reported in Eckstein (ed.), *Internal Wars*.
54. See I. Horowitz, *The Rise and Fall of Project Camelot*, and by the same author, *Foundations of Political Sociology*, pp. 414–30.
55. The Historical and Comparative Task Force Report to the Commission is published as Graham and Gurr (eds), *Violence in America*.
56. Bell, *Resistance and Revolution*, pp. 1–2.
57. See e.g. Easton, 'The New Revolution in Political Science'. Even negative responses helped the study of revolutions. It appears that Tullock, who was highly critical of the student revolt, began his work on 'economic' theories of revolutions in order to provide an academic critique of the motives for student radicalism. See 'The Paradox of Revolution', p. 89.
58. Cohen, op. cit.
59. Freeman, op. cit.

60. Stone, 'Theories of Revolution'.
61. Zagorin, op. cit.

CHAPTER 1: SOCIOLOGICAL THEORIES OF REVOLUTIONS

1. A good discussion of the distinctiveness of sociological approaches among those used in the social sciences is to be found in Bottomore and Nisbet (eds), *A History of Sociological Analysis*, pp. vii–xvi.
2. The differences between these are set out in Lipset, *Revolution and Counter-Revolution*, pp. 121–58.
3. Durkheim, *The Division of Labour in Society*.
4. Parsons, *The Social System*.
5. Merton, *Social Theory and Social Structure*.
6. Johnson, *Revolutionary Change*.
7. Barrington Moore, *Social Origins of Dictatorship and Democracy*.
8. Skocpol, *States and Social Revolutions*.
9. Gouldner, *The Coming Crisis of Western Sociology*.
10. Smelser, *Theory of Collective Behaviour*.
11. Freeman, 'Review Article: Theories of Revolution', pp. 340–5.
12. Johnson, op. cit.
13. Ibid., p. 20.
14. Ibid., p. 45.
15. Ibid., p. 41.
16. Ibid., p. 42.
17. Parsons, op. cit., pp. 26–35
18. Weber's definition was a 'human community that (successfully) claims the monopoly of the legitimate use of physical force within a given territory': see Gerth and Mills (eds), *From Max Weber*, p. 78.
19. Johnson, op. cit., p. 52.
20. Ibid., p. 1.
21. Ibid., pp. 27–33.
22. Ibid., p. 91.
23. Ibid., p. 97.
24. Ibid., p. 91.
25. Ibid., p. 132.
26. See Chapter 3.
27. Russell, *Rebellion, Revolution and Armed Force*.
28. Freeman, op. cit., pp. 341–5.
29. Eckstein, 'On the Etiology of Internal Wars', pp. 147–51.
30. See for example L. Stone, 'The English Revolution' in Forster and Greene (eds), *Preconditions of Revolution in Early Modern Europe*, particularly p. 65.
31. Stone, 'Theories of Revolution', p. 166.
32. McLellan, *Marxism After Marx*, p. 1.
33. See in particular the section on the Paris Manuscripts in D. McLellan, *Karl Marx*, pp. 104–27, and K. Marx, *Grundrisse*.
34. An excellent discussion of this is contained in M. Evans, *Karl Marx*.
35. See for discussion in McLellan, *Marxism After Marx*, pp. 66–7.

36. Thus, for example, Marx wrote disparagingly of the 'idiocy of rural life' (see K. Marx and F. Engels, *The Communist Manifesto*, p. 84) and noted that peasants were unable to combine as a class (see Marx, 18th Brumaire, quoted in T. Bottomore and M. Reubel, *Karl Marx*, p. 196) and implement radical change.
37. See e.g. the discussion of the work of Dahrendorf, Aron and Ossowski in Giddens, *The Class Structure of the Advanced Societies*, pp. 53–8.
38. The two outstanding, if different, contributions of this kind were Milliband, *The State in Capitalist Society*, and Poulantzas, *Political Power and Social Classes*.
39. '. . . the bourgeoisie has, at last, since the establishment of Modern Industry and of the world market, conquered for itself, in the modern representative state, exclusive political sway. The executive of the modern state is but a committee for managing the common affairs of the whole bourgeoisie', *Communist Manifesto*, p. 82.
40. See Schram, *The Political Thought of Mao Tse-Tung*, pp. 236–64.
41. Barrington Moore later claimed that he had only utilized Marx's theory in so far as it applied to the analysis of the role of the upper classes in modernization. See 'A Reply to Rothman', p. 81. Barrington Moore did produce a second volume which purported to describe lower-class behaviour, but this was less an empirical work than one of normative political theory. See *Injustice: The Social Bases of Obedience and Revolt*.
42. Barrington Moore, *Social Origins*, p. vii.
43. For an exposition of this, see Ryan, *The Philosophy of the Social Sciences*, p. 224 especially.
44. Barrington Moore, *Social Origins*, p. xii.
45. Skocpol, 'A Critical Review of Barrington Moore's *Social Origins of Dictatorship and Democracy*', pp. 1–34
46. As for example in the contrast between the 'little workshop of the patriarchial master' and the modern factory where 'masses of labourers are organized like soldiers. As privates of the industrial army they are placed under the command of a perfect hierarchy of officers and sergeants'. See *Communist Manifesto*, pp. 87–8.
47. Barrington Moore, *Social Origins*, p. 315.
48. Ibid.; for China see pp. 174–8; for Russia, pp. 177, 415.
49. Ibid., pp. 181–2.
50. Ibid., pp. 201, 213.
51. Ibid., p. 206.
52. Ibid., p. 475.
53. Ibid.; for Japan see pp. 228–318; for Germany see pp. 435–40.
54. Ibid., p. 433.
55. Ibid., pp. 14–20.
56. Ibid., pp. 152–5.
57. Ibid., pp. 104–6.
58. Ibid., p. 426.
59. Ibid., pp. 7, 14.
60. Ibid., pp. 40, 56–63.
61. Ibid., p. 136.
62. Rothman, 'Barrington Moore and the Dialectics of Revolution: An Essay

Review', p. 66; Femia, 'Barrington Moore and the Preconditions for Democracy', pp. 32-3.
63. Rothman, op. cit., p. 66.
64. Cobban, *The Social Interpretation of the French Revolution*.
65. Skocpol, 'A Critical Review of Barrington Moore's *Social Origins of Dictatorship and Democracy*', p. 24.
66. Ibid.
67. Skocpol, *States and Social Revolutions*, pp. 100-4, Rothman, op. cit., pp. 67-8.
68. Rothman, op. cit., pp. 79-80.
69. Ibid., p. 62.
70. Barrington Moore, *Social Origins*, pp. ix-x.
71. Skocpol, *States and Social Revolutions*, p. 4.
72. Ibid., pp. 4-5.
73. Ibid., pp. 14-18.
74. Ibid., p. 117.
75. Ibid., pp. 47-67, 118-28.
76. Ibid., pp. 67-80, 147-54.
77. Ibid., pp. 94-9, 128-40.
78. Ibid., pp. 100-4.
79. Ibid., pp. 104-9, 144-7.
80. Ibid., pp. 140-4.
81. Ibid., pp. 161-73.
82. Ibid., pp. 282-3.
83. Ibid., p. 181.
84. Ibid., p. 282.
85. Ibid., pp. 287-93.
86. Changes in the international environment were included in Johnson's model, see *Revolutionary Change*, pp. 56-70, and have been discussed by others, see e.g. Deutsch, 'External Involvement in Internal War'.
87. Skocpol, *States and Social Revolutions*, pp. 14-16.
88. Ibid., pp. 284-5.
89. Lewis, *The Politics of Revolt*, pp. 13-36.
90. Wolf, *Peasant Wars*, p. 120.
91. Ibid., p. 154.
92. Hinton, *Fanshen*.
93. McKenzie, *Politics and Social Science*, pp. 81-3, 111-12.

CHAPTER 2: SOCIO-PSYCHOLOGICAL THEORIES OF REVOLUTIONS

1. Le Bon, *The Psychology of Revolution*.
2. Ellwood, 'A Psychological Theory of Revolutions', pp. 49-59.
3. These are summarized in Rejai with Phillips, *Leaders of Revolution*, pp. 45-52.
4. Perhaps the strongest statement of the case for behaviouralism was contained in Eulau, *The Behavioural Persuasion in Politics*. See also Kirkpatrick, 'The Impact of the Behavioural Approach on Traditional Political Science'.

5. Eckstein, 'On the Etiology of Internal Wars', pp. 143–5.
6. Festinger, *The Theory of Cognitive Dissonance*.
7. Ibid., p. 3.
8. Geschwender, 'Explorations in the Theory of Revolutions and Social Movements'.
9. Ibid., p. 128.
10. Schwartz, 'A Theory of Revolutionary Behaviour', pp. 109–32.
11. Brinton, *The Anatomy of Revolution*.
12. Three of the best-known 'mass society' theorists are Arendt, *The Origins of Totalitarianism*, Fromm, *The Fear of Freedom*, and Kornhauser, *The Politics of Mass Society*. For expositions and critiques see Cohen, *Theories of Revolution*, pp. 146–72 and Giner, *Mass Society*, especially pp. 136–58.
13. Dollard, Doob, Miller, Mowrer and Sears, *Frustration and Aggression*.
14. Ibid., p. 11.
15. Davies, 'Towards a Theory of Revolution' and 'The "J" Curve of Rising and Declining Satisfactions'.
16. Davies, 'Towards a Theory of Revolution', p. 6.
17. Ibid., p. 10.
18. Tanter and Midlarsky, 'A Theory of Revolution'.
19. Ibid., p. 267.
20. Lipset, *Political Man*, pp. 55–6
21. Russett, 'Inequality and Instability: The Relation of Land Tenure to Politics'.
22. Bwy, 'Dimensions of Social Conflict in Latin America'.
23. Ibid., p. 275.
24. Rummel, 'Dimensions of Conflict Behaviour Within and Between Nations' and 'Dimensions of Conflict Behaviour Within Nations 1946–59'.
25. Tanter, 'Dimensions of Conflict Behaviour Within and Between Nations 1958–60'.
26. Gurr, *Why Men Rebel*.
27. Ibid., pp. 3–4.
28. Eckstein, 'On the Etiology of Internal Wars', pp. 156–9.
29. Gurr, *Why Men Rebel*, p. 24.
30. Deutsch, 'Social Mobilization and Political Development'.
31. I. and R. Feierabend, 'Aggressive Behaviours Within Polities 1948–62'.
32. Wertheim, *Evolution and Revolution*, pp. 192–3.
33. In which case the 'Reign of Terror' could be construed as an attempt by the revolutionaries to repress opposition, with the onset of Thermidor reflecting the ultimate success of this stage in the development of the revolution. See Brinton, op. cit., pp. 176–236.
34. Reported in Gurr, 'A Causal Model of Civil Strife'.
35. Milgram, *Obedience to Authority*, pp. 165–8.
36. Ibid., pp. 123–35.
37. Lupsha, 'Explanations of Political Violence: Some Psychological Theories vs. Indignation'.

38. Bachrach and Baratz, *Power and Poverty*, especially pp. 105–6.
39. Thomas, *Cuba*, pp. 932–3.
40. Ibid., pp. 996–1047.
41. Eckstein, op. cit., pp. 134, 148–51.
42. The arguments against the behaviouralist approach were well summarized in Easton, 'The New Revolution in Political Science'.
43. Gurr, 'A Causal Model of Civil Strife', pp. 312–13.

CHAPTER 3: ECONOMIC THEORIES OF REVOLUTIONS

1. Schumpeter, *Capitalism, Socialism and Democracy*, p. 262.
2. See for example Lazarsfeld, Gaudet and Berelson, *The People's Choice*, and Runciman, *Social Science and Political Theory*, pp. 89–92.
3. See Campbell, Converse, Miller and Stokes, *The American Voter* and Runciman, op. cit., pp. 93–5.
4. Mill, *Representative Government*, pp. 242–56.
5. Downs, *An Economic Theory of Democracy*.
6. Olson, *The Logic of Collective Action*.
7. Ireland, 'The Rationale of Revolt', pp. 49–66.
8. In that he posited that voters would still vote because they wished to secure the long-run future of democracy as a political system. See Downs, op. cit., pp. 266–71, and for a critical comment, Barry, *Sociologists, Economists and Democracy*, pp. 20–3.
9. Tullock, 'The Paradox of Revolution', pp. 87–100.
10. Silver, 'Political Revolutions and Repression: An Economic Approach', pp. 63–71.
11. Olson, op. cit.
12. Tullock, op. cit., p. 89.
13. Ibid.
14. Tullock, *The Social Dilemma: The Economics of War and Revolution*, pp. 4–60.
15. Tullock, 'The Paradox of Revolution', p. 95.
16. Silver, op. cit., pp. 63–4.
17. If both of these terms were zero, the Tullock equations would reduce to the pay-offs being determined by the entertainment value minus the sum of the private costs imposed by the regime on the individual and the chances of various types of injuries (e.g. $G_r = P_r = E - (P_i + L_w I_r)$). While public goods did not enter into this equation, neither did private benefits.
18. Downs, op. cit., pp. 4–8. This was criticized by Riker and Ordeshook in 'A Theory of the Calculus of Voting', especially p. 25, who took Tullock and Silver's position, but their defence of the wider definition was demolished by Barry, op. cit., pp. 15–16.
19. Plamenatz, *Democracy and Illusion*, pp. 148–79.
20. The literature on revolutionary leaders is summarized in Rejai with Phillips, *Leaders of Revolution* and stresses only psychological and sociological motives for becoming revolutionaries.

CHAPTER 4: POLITICAL THEORIES OF REVOLUTIONS

1. For discussions of Machiavelli's theory in the context of revolutions see Bell, *Resistance and Revolution*, pp. 22–3, Arendt, *On Revolution*, pp. 35–9.
2. Eckstein, 'On the Etiology of Internal Wars', pp. 136–7.
3. Ibid., p. 137.
4. Huntington, *Political Order in Changing Societies*.
5. Tilly, 'Does Modernization Breed Revolution?', 'Revolutions and Collective Violence' and *From Mobilization to Revolution*.
6. This is well summarized by one of its detractors, Lipset, in *Political Man*, especially p. 78.
7. Ibid.
8. Olson, 'Rapid Growth as a Destabilizing Force', p. 529.
9. Huntington, op. cit., pp. 32–9.
10. Quoted in Olson, op. cit., p. 529.
11. Kornhauser, *The Politics of Mass Society*, pp. 119–66.
12. Olson, op. cit.
13. Deutsch, 'Social Mobilization and Political Development'.
14. Huntington, op. cit., pp. 8–12.
15. Ibid.
16. Ibid., p. 9.
17. Rostow, *Politics and the Stages of Growth*, pp. 11–12.
18. Deutsch, op. cit.
19. Huntington, op. cit., p. 34.
20. Ibid., p. 11.
21. Ibid., p. 86.
22. Ibid., pp. 1–8.
23. Ibid., p. 264.
24. Ibid.
25. Ibid., pp. 277–8.
26. Ibid., p. 275.
27. Ibid., p. 273.
28. Pettee, *The Process of Revolution*, quoted in Huntington, op. cit., pp. 267–8.
29. Gillis, 'Political Decay and the European Revolutions 1789–1848'.
30. Tilly, 'Does Modernization Breed Revolution?'.
31. Russell, *Rebellion, Revolution and Armed Force*.
32. This evidence is summarized and additional confirmatory data is presented in Feierabend and Feierabend, 'Aggressive Behaviours Within Polities'.
33. Sorokin, *Social and Cultural Dynamics III: Fluctuation of Social Relationships, War and Revolution*.
34. Tilly, 'Revolutions and Collective Violence', pp. 499–500.
35. Tilly, *From Mobilization to Revolution*, pp. 52–5.
36. Ibid., p. 52.
37. Ibid.
38. Ibid., p 5.
39. Ibid., p. 198.
40. Ibid., p. 191.
41. Amann, 'Revolution: A Redefinition'.

42. Bell, op. cit., pp. 130–6.
43. Russell, op. cit.
44. See e.g. Finer, *The Man on Horseback*, pp. 32, 113–15.
45. Ibid., pp. 21, 87–8, 115, and Johnson, *The Role of the Military in Underdeveloped Countries*, p. 127.
46. See Skocpol, *States and Social Revolutions*, pp. 10–11.

CHAPTER 5: SOCIAL SCIENCE AND REVOLUTIONS

1. Button, *Black Violence*, pp. 4–9.
2. Wolin, 'The Politics of the Study of Revolutions', pp. 343–59.
3. Dunn, *Modern Revolutions*.
4. Ibid., pp. 241–3.
5. Barrington Moore, *Injustice: The Social Bases of Obedience and Revolt*.
6. MacIntyre, 'Ideology, Social Science and Revolution', pp. 321–42.
7. Brinton, *The Anatomy of Revolution*.
8. Wolf, *Peasant Wars*.
9. Mackenzie, *Politics and Social Science*, pp. 306, 385.

Bibliography

T. Adorno, E. Frenkel-Brunswik, D. Levinson and R. Nevitt Sandford, *The Authoritarian Personality* (New York: Harper and Row, 1950).
G. Almond and S. Verba, *The Civic Culture* (Boston: Little, Brown, 1973).
P. Amann, 'Revolution: A Redefinition', *Political Science Quarterly,* 77 (1962), pp. 36–53.
H. Arendt, *The Origins of Totalitarianism* (London: Allen and Unwin, 1967).
H. Arendt, *On Revolution* (Harmondsworth: Penguin, 1973).
P. Bachrach and M. Baratz, *Power and Poverty* (London: Oxford University Press, 1970).
Barrington Moore Jnr, *The Social Origins of Dictatorship and Democracy* (Harmondsworth: Penguin, 1969)
Barrington Moore Jnr, *Reflections on the Causes of Human Misery* (London: Allen Lane, 1972).
Barrington Moore Jnr, *Injustice: The Social Bases of Obedience and Revolt* (London: Macmillan, 1978).
Barrington Moore Jnr, 'A Reply to Rothman', *American Political Science Review*, 64 (1970), pp. 61–82.
B. Barry, *Sociologists, Economists and Democracy* (London: Collier-Macmillan, 1970).
D. Bell, *The End of Ideology* (New York: Free Press, 1962).
D. Bell, *Resistance and Revolution* (Boston: Houghton Mifflin, 1973).
T. Bottomore and R. Nisbet (eds), *A History of Sociological Analysis* (London: Heinemann, 1979).
T. Bottomore and M. Reubel, *Karl Marx: Selected Writings in Sociology and Social Philosophy* (London: Pelican, 1971).
C. Brinton, *The Anatomy of Revolution* (New York: Vintage, 1965).
D. Brogan, *The Price of Revolution* (London: Hamish Hamilton, 1951).
J. Button, *Black Violence* (Princeton University Press, 1978).
D. Bwy, 'Dimensions of Social Conflict in Latin America' in Davies (ed.) (1971) pp. 274–91.
P. Calvert, *A Study of Revolution* (London: Oxford University Press, 1970).
P. Calvert, *Revolution* (London: Pall Mall, 1970).
A. Campbell, P. Converse, W. Miller and D. Stokes, *The American Voter* (London: John Wiley, 1964).
K. Chorley, *Armies and the Art of Revolution* (Boston: Beacon Press, 1973).
A. Cobban, *The Social Interpretation of the French Revolution* (Cambridge University Press, 1971).

Bibliography

A. Cohen, *Theories of Revolution: An Introduction* (London: Nelson, 1975).
B. Crick (ed.), *Machiavelli: The Discourses* (London: Pelican, 1970).
J. Davies, 'Towards a Theory of Revolution', *American Sociological Review*, 27 (1962), pp. 5–18.
J. Davies, 'The "J" Curve of Rising and Declining Satisfactions as a Cause of Some Great Revolutions and a Contained Rebellion', in Graham and Gurr (eds) (1969) pp. 671–709.
J. Davies (ed.), *When Men Revolt and Why* (New York: Free Press, 1971).
A. De Tocqueville, *The Old Regime and the French Revolution* (New York: Doubleday, 1955).
K. Deutsch, 'External Involvement in Internal Wars', in Eckstein (ed.) (1964) pp. 100–10.
K. Deutsch, 'Social Mobilization and Political Development', *American Political Science Review*, 55 (1961), pp. 493–514.
I. Deutscher, 'The French Revolution and the Russian Revolution: Some Suggestive Analogies', *World Politics*, 4 (1952), pp. 369–81.
J. Dollard, L. Doob, N. Miller, O. Mowrer and R. Sears, *Frustration and Aggression* (New Haven: Yale University Press, 1974).
A. Downs, *An Economic Theory of Democracy* (New York: Harper and Row, 1957).
J. Dunn, *Modern Revolutions* (London: Cambridge University Press, 1972).
E. Durkheim, *The Division of Labour in Society* (New York: Free Press, 1964).
D. Easton, 'The New Revolution in Political Science', *American Political Science Review*, 63 (1969), pp. 1051–61.
H. Eckstein (ed.), *Internal War* (New York: Free Press, 1964).
H. Eckstein, 'On the Etiology of Internal Wars', *History and Theory*, 4 (1965), pp. 133–63.
L. Edwards, *The Natural History of Revolutions* (Chicago University Press, 1970).
J. Elliott, 'Revolts in the Spanish Monarchy', in Forster and Greene (eds) (1970), pp. 109–30.
C. Ellwood, 'A Psychological Theory of Revolutions', *American Journal of Sociology*, 11 (1905), pp. 49–59.
H. Eulau, *The Behavioural Persuasion in Politics* (New York: Random House, 1963).
M. Evans, *Karl Marx* (London: Allen and Unwin, 1975).
I. Feierabend and R. Feierabend, 'Aggressive Behaviours Within Polities 1948-62', *Journal of Conflict Resolution*, 10 (1966), pp. 249–71.
J. Femia, 'Barrington Moore and the Preconditions for Democracy', *British Journal of Political Science*, 2 (1972), pp. 21–46.
L. Festinger, *The Theory of Cognitive Dissonance* (Stanford University Press, 1967).
S. Finer, *The Man on Horseback* (London: Pall Mall, 1962).
R. Forster and J. Greene (eds), *Preconditions of Revolution in Early Modern Europe* (Baltimore: Johns Hopkins Press, 1970).
M. Freeman, *Edmund Burke and the Critique of Political Radicalism* (London: Blackwell, 1980).
M. Freeman, 'Theories of Revolution', *British Journal of Political Science*, 2 (1972), pp. 339–59.
E. Fromm, *The Fear of Freedom* (London: Routledge and Kegan Paul, 1942).
H. Gerth and C. Wright-Mills (eds), *From Max Weber* (London: Routledge and Kegan Paul, 1970).

J. Geschwender, 'Explorations in the Theory of Revolutions and Social Movements', *Social Forces*, 42 (1968), pp. 127-35.
A. Giddens, *The Class Structure of the Advanced Societies* (London: Hutchinson, 1973).
J. Gillis, 'Political Decay and the European Revolutions 1789-1848', *World Politics*, 22 (1970), pp. 344-70.
S. Giner, *Mass Society* (London: Martin Robertson, 1976).
L. Gottshalk, 'Causes of Revolution', *American Journal of Sociology*, 50 (1944), pp. 1-8.
A. Gouldner, *The Coming Crisis of Western Sociology* (London: Heinemann, 1971).
H. Graham and T. Gurr (eds), *Violence in America* (New York: Signet Books, 1969).
T. H. Greene, *Comparative Revolutionary Movements* (Englewood Cliffs, NJ: Prentice-Hall, 1974).
F. Greenstein and N. Polsby (eds), *Handbook of Political Science*, Vol. 3 (Reading, Mass: Addison-Wesley, 1975).
F. Gross, *The Seizure of Power in a Century of Revolutions* (New York: Philosophical Library, 1958).
T. Gurr, 'Psychological Factors in Civil Violence', *World Politics*, 20 (1968), pp. 245-78.
T. Gurr, 'A Causal Model of Civil Strife', *American Political Science Review*, 62 (1968), pp. 1104-24.
T. Gurr, *Why Men Rebel* (Princeton University Press, 1971).
A. Hatto, '"Revolution": An Enquiry into the Usefulness of a Historical Term', *Mind*, LVIII (1947), pp. 495-517.
W. Hinton, *Fanshen* (London: Pelican, 1972).
R. Hopper, 'The Revolutionary Process', *Social Forces*, 28 (1950), pp. 270-9.
I. Horowitz, *The Rise and Fall of Project Camelot: Studies in the Relationship Between the Social Sciences and Practical Politics* (Cambridge, Mass.: MIT Press, 1967).
I. Horowitz, *Foundations of Political Sociology* (New York: Harper and Row, 1972).
S. Huntington, *Political Order in Changing Societies* (Yale University Press, 1971).
T. Ireland, 'The Rationale of Revolt', *Papers in Non-Market Decision-Making*, 1 (1967), pp. 49-66.
C. Johnson, *Revolutionary Change* (University of London Press, 1968).
J. Johnson, *The Role of the Military in Underdeveloped Countries* (Princeton University Press, 1962).
A. Kirkpatrick, 'The Impact of the Behavioural Approach upon Traditional Political Science', in Ranney (ed.) (1963) pp. 1-30.
F. Kort, 'The Quantification of Aristotle's Theory of Revolution', *American Political Science Review*, 46 (1952), pp. 486-93.
W. Kornhauser, *The Politics of Mass Society* (London: Routledge and Kegan Paul, 1960).
K. Kumar, *Revolution* (London: Weidenfeld and Nicolson, 1971).
H. Lasswell and A. Kaplan, *Power and Society* (New Haven: Yale University Press, 1955).
P. Lazarsfeld, H. Gaudet and B. Berelson, *The People's Choice* (New York: Columbia University Press, 1948).
G. Le Bon, *The Psychology of Revolution* (New York: Putnams, 1913).
C. Leiden and K. Schmitt, *The Politics of Violence: Revolution in the Modern World*

(Englewood Cliffs, NJ: Prentice-Hall, 1968).
P. Lewis, *The Politics of Revolt* (Milton Keynes: Open University Press, 1974).
S. M. Lipset, *The First New Nation* (London: Heinemann, 1964).
S. M. Lipset, *Political Man* (London: Heinemann, 1969).
S. M. Lipset, *Revolution and Counter-Revolution* (London: Heinemann, 1969).
P. Lupsha, 'Explanations of Political Violence: Some Psychological Theories vs. Indignation', *Politics and Society*, 2 (1971), pp. 89–104.
A. MacIntyre, 'Ideology, Social Science and Revolution', *Comparative Politics*, 5 (1973), pp. 321–42.
W. Mackenzie, *Politics and Social Science* (London: Pelican, 1969).
K. Marx, *Grundrisse* (London: Pelican, in association with the New Left Review, 1973).
K. Marx and F. Engels, *The Communist Manifesto* (London: Pelican, 1967).
D. McLellan, *Karl Marx: His Life and Thought* (London: Macmillan, 1973).
D. McLellan, *Marxism after Marx* (London: Macmillan, 1979).
R. Merton, *Social Theory and Social Structure* (New York: Free Press, 1967).
S. Milgram, *Obedience to Authority* (London: Tavistock, 1974).
J. S. Mill, *Representative Government* (London: Dent, 1910).
R. Milliband, *The State in Capitalist Society* (London: Quartet, 1973).
S. Neumann, 'The Structure and Strategy of Revolutions: 1848 and 1948', *Journal of Politics*, 11 (1949), pp. 532–44.
M. Olson, *The Logic of Collective Action* (Boston: Harvard University Press, 1965).
M. Olson, 'Rapid Growth as a Destabilizing Force', *Journal of Economic History*, 23 (1963), pp. 529–52.
T. Paine, *The Rights of Man* (London: Pelican, 1971).
R. Palmer, 'The World Revolution in the West', *Political Science Quarterly*, 69 (1954), pp. 1–14.
T. Parsons, *The Social System* (New York: Free Press, 1964).
T. Parsons and E. Shils, *Towards a General Theory of Action: Theoretical Foundations for the Social Sciences* (New York: Harper and Row, 1962).
G. Pettee, *The Process of Revolution* (New York: Harper, 1938).
K. Popper, *The Open Society and Its Enemies*, Vol. 1, Plato (London: Routledge and Kegan Paul, 1969).
J. Plamenatz, *Democracy and Illusion* (London: Longmans, 1973).
N. Poulantzas, *Political Power and Social Classes* (London: Verso, 1978).
L. Pye, 'The Roots of Insurgency and the Commencement of Rebellions', in Eckstein (ed.) (1964) pp. 157–79.
A. Ranney (ed.), *Essays in the Behavioural Study of Politics* (Urbana: University of Illinois Press, 1963).
M. Rejai with K. Phillips, *Leaders of Revolution* (London: Sage, 1979).
K. Riezler, 'On the Psychology of Modern Revolutions', *Social Research*, 10 (1943), pp. 320–36.
W. Riker and P. Ordeshook, 'A Theory of the Calculus of Voting', *American Political Science Review*, 62 (1968), pp. 25–42.
W. Rostow, *Politics and the Stages of Growth* (London: Cambridge University Press, 1971).
S. Rothman, 'Barrington Moore and the Dialectics of Revolution: An Essay Review', *American Political Science Review*, 64 (1970), pp. 61–82.
R. Rummel, 'Dimensions of Conflict Behaviour Within and Between Nations', *General Systems Yearbook*, VIII (1963), pp. 1–50.

R. Rummel, 'Dimensions of Conflict Behaviour Within Nations 1946–59', *Journal of Conflict Resolution*, X (1966), pp. 65–73.
W. Runciman, *Social Science and Political Theory* (London: Cambridge University Press, 1971).
D. Russell, *Rebellion, Revolution and Armed Force* (New York: Academic Press, 1974).
B. Russett, 'Inequality and Instability: The Relation of Land Tenure to Politics', *World Politics*, 16 (1964), pp. 442–54.
A. Ryan, *The Philosophy of the Social Sciences* (London: Macmillan, 1970).
S. Schram, *The Political Thought of Mao Tse-tung* (London: Pelican, 1969).
J. Schumpeter, *Capitalism, Socialism and Democracy* (London: George Allen and Unwin, 1966).
D. Schwartz, 'A Theory of Revolutionary Behaviour', in J. Davies (ed.) (1971), pp. 109–33.
M. Silver, 'Political Revolutions and Repression: An Economic Approach', *Public Choice*, XIV (1974), pp. 63–71.
T. Skocpol, 'A Critical Review of Barrington Moore's *Social Origins of Dictatorship and Democracy*', *Politics and Society*, 4 (1973), pp. 1–34.
T. Skocpol, *States and Social Revolutions* (London: Cambridge University Press, 1979).
N. Smelser, *Theory of Collective Behaviour* (London: Routledge and Kegan Paul, 1961).
P. Sorokin, *The Sociology of Revolution* (New York: Lippincott, 1925).
P. Sorokin, *Social and Cultural Dynamics III: Fluctuation of Social Relationships, War and Revolution* (New York: Bedminster, 1962).
L. Stone, 'Theories of Revolution', *World Politics*, 18 (1966), pp. 159–76.
R. Tanter, 'Dimensions of Conflict Behaviour Within and Between Nations 1958–60', *Peace Research Society Papers*, III (1965), pp. 159–84.
R. Tanter and M. Midlarsky, 'A Theory of Revolution', *Journal of Conflict Resolution*, XI (1967), pp. 264–80.
H. Thomas, *Cuba or the Pursuit of Freedom* (London: Eyre and Spottiswoode, 1971).
C. Tilly, 'Does Modernization Breed Revolution?', *Comparative Politics*, 5 (1973), pp. 425–47.
C. Tilly, 'Revolutions and Collective Violence', in Greenstein and Polsby (eds) (1975).
C. Tilly, *From Mobilization to Revolution* (Reading, Mass.: Addison-Wesley, 1978).
G. Tullock, 'The Paradox of Revolution', *Public Choice*, XI (1971), pp. 87–100.
G. Tullock, *The Social Dilemma: The Economics of War and Revolution* (Blackburg, Virginia: University Publications, 1974).
A. Wallace, 'Revitalization Movements', *American Anthropologist*, 58 (1956), pp. 264–81.
M. Waltzer, *Revolution of the Saints* (Cambridge, Mass.: Harvard University Press, 1965).
W. Wertheim, *Evolution and Revolution* (Harmondsworth: Penguin, 1974).
E. Wolf, *Peasant Wars of the Twentieth Century* (London: Faber, 1971).
S. Wolin, 'The Politics of the Study of Revolutions', *Comparative Politics*, 5 (1973), pp. 343–59.
D. Yoder, 'Current Definitions of Revolution', *American Journal of Sociology*, 32 (1926), pp. 433–41.

P. Zagorin, 'Theories of Revolution in Contemporary Historiography', *Political Science Quarterly*, 88 (1973), pp. 23–51.

Index

Algerian revolution, 46, 153
American Civil War, 30, 32–3
American Political Science Association, 7
American War of Independence, 3, 25, 29, 105
Amman, P., 135
Angolan revolution, 46
Argentina, 104
Aristotle, 53

Barrington Moore Jnr, 11, 24–32, 51, 151, 153, 155, 157
Batista, F., 87
Bell, D., 7–8, 135
Black Power, 105
Bolivian Revolution, 46
Bolshevik party, 112
Boxer Rebellion, 105
Brinton, C., 4, 56, 78, 157
Brogan, D., 4
Burke, E., 3
Button, J., 152
Bwy, D., 68–71, 84, 85, 91, 151, 157

Castro, F., 88
Chinese Communist Party, 44, 45, 49
Chinese Revolution, 5, 25, 28, 32–3, 36, 38–9, 43–6, 47, 48–9, 108, 121, 123, 124, 153
Chorley, K., 4
Cobban, A., 32
Cuban Revolution, 5, 7, 18, 20, 46, 66–8, 84, 108–9, 121, 153

Davies, J., 61–5, 70, 72, 84, 85, 88, 89, 91, 151, 157
De Gaulle, C., 66, 96
De Tocqueville, A., 3, 62, 103

Deutsch, K., 116
Deutscher, I., 4
Dollard, J., 60
Doob, L., 60
Dorr's Rebellion, 64, 87
Downs, A., 94, 96, 109–10
Dunn, R., 153, 156, 157
Durkheim, E., 10

Eckstein, H., 4–5, 20, 52, 90, 114
Edwards, L., 4
Egyptian coup of 1952, 64, 87
Ellwood, C., 4, 52
English Civil War, 1, 3, 25, 29, 31–3, 36, 41, 43
English 'revolutions' of 1204–68 and 1450–87, 104
Ethiopia, 46

Festinger, L., 53–4
France
  Revolution of 1789, 3, 25, 29, 32, 36, 38, 41, 43–4, 47, 51, 64–5, 108, 121, 123, 125, 128, 154, 157
  Revolution of 1830, 123
  Revolution of 1848, 123
  Coup of 1958, 66, 96
Freeman, M., 4, 12

Germany, 25, 29, 32, 36, 40–1, 42, 104
Geschwender, J., 54–6, 84, 89, 151
Gillis, J., 125, 127, 150, 154
Gottshalk, L., 4
Guinea-Bissau, 46
Gurr, T., 71–84, 89, 91, 125, 128, 130, 131, 149, 151, 157

Hatto, A., 1, 4
Hegel, G., 3

Index

Hopper, R., 5
Hungary
  Revolution of 1917–19, 104
  Revolution of 1956, 48
Huntington, S., 116–30, 149, 150, 151, 152, 154, 156

India, 25–7, 34
Ireland, T., 94, 106

Jacobins, 147
Japan, 25, 29, 32, 36, 39–40, 42
Johnson, C., 10, 51, 127, 152, 155

Kaplan, A., 4
Korea, 123
Kornhauser, A., 116
Kuomingtang, 49

Lasswell, H., 4
Le Bon, G., 4, 52
Lenin, V., 155
Lewis, P., 48
Lipset, S., 66
Locke, J., 3

Machiavelli, 3, 114, 149
Mackenzie, W., 51, 158
Mao Tse-Tung, 24, 155
Marx, K., 3, 11, 21–4, 61–2
McIntyre, A., 156–7
McLellan, D., 21
Merton, R., 10
Mexican Revolution, 46, 121, 123, 153
Midlarsky, M., see Tanter, R.
Milgram, S., 85–6
Mill, J. S., 94
Moncada barracks, 88
Mowrer, O., 60
Mozambique, 46

National Commission on Causes and Prevention of Violence, 7
Nazi party, 112
Neumann, S., 4
Nien rebellion, 49

Olson, M., 94, 116
Ottoman Empire, 123

Paine, T., 155
Palmer, R., 4
Paris Commune, 104
Parsons, T., 5, 10
Peron, J., 104
Pettee, G., 4, 122
Plato, 3
Poland, 48
Prussia, 36, 40, 125
Pye, L., 5

Qajar dynasty, 123

Revolutions
  economic theories of, 93–111
  importance in twentieth century, 3–4
  growth of academic interest in, 6–8
  neglect of by social scientists, 4–6
  origins of word, 1–3
  political theories of, 116–49
  sociological theories of, 10–50
  socio-psychological theories of, 51–84
Riezler, K., 4
Rothman, S., 33
Rummel, R., 69
Russell, D., 18, 125, 127, 154
Russia
  in 1905, 91
  Revolution of 1917, 3, 22, 25, 28–9, 36, 38–9, 41, 43, 45, 47, 64, 87, 91–2, 104, 108, 121, 123, 153

Schumpeter, J., 93
Schwartz, D., 56–60, 84, 85, 89, 148, 151
Sears, D., 60
Self-Anchoring Striving Scale, 69
Sicily, 126
Silver, M., 96, 102–5, 106, 109, 110, 113, 151, 154
Skocpol, T., 11, 25–6, 32, 34–50, 51, 150, 151, 153, 157
Smelser, N., 12
Sorokin, P., 4, 126
South Africa, 15, 18, 20, 126, 129, 157
Syngman Rhee, 123

Taiping Rebellion, 49

Tanter, R., 69
  with Midlarsky, M., 65–8, 84, 85, 87, 88–9, 91, 148, 151, 157
Thucydides, 3
Tilly, C., 115, 125, 126, 127, 128–54
Tullock, G., 96–102, 106, 109–10, 113, 151, 154
Turkey, 104, 153

Vietnam, 3, 7, 46, 124, 153

Wallace, A., 4
Wertheim, W., 73
Wolf, E., 157

Yoder, D., 4
Yugoslavia, 46, 153